TAROT FORECASTS 2018

Karmel Nair was born a Catholic, is married to a Hindu and practises the Buddhist way of life. She worked in a media house and was a successful radio jockey with leading radio stations before she embarked on a career in tarot fortune-telling. It was through a chance meeting that she encountered tarot. As she delved deeper into the tarot world, Karmel discovered her intuitive powers. Tarot led her to what she describes as the most magnificent discovery of her life – Vipassana (the study and practice of mindfulness), which helped her deal with the persistent vacuum she felt in her life.

Equipped with a master's degree in psychotherapy and her skills as a tarot reader, Karmel found herself in a position to help people know what the future had in store for them, and to mitigate the negatives through corrective measures.

Tarot Forecasts 2018 is not only a book about the future but also a medium to change it through spiritual realization by harnessing the power of the being within us.

TAROT FORECASTS 2018

KARMEL NAIR

First published in India in 2017 by Harper Element
An imprint of HarperCollins *Publishers*

P-ISBN: 978-93-5277-084-7
E-ISBN: 978-93-5277-081-6

2 4 6 8 10 9 7 5 3 1

HarperCollins *Publishers*
A-75, Sector 57, Noida, Uttar Pradesh 201301, India
1 London Bridge Street, London, SE1 9GF, United Kingdom
2 Bloor Street East, Toronto, Ontario M4W 1A8, Canada
Lvl 13, 201 Elizabeth Street (PO Box A565, NSW, 1235), Sydney
NSW 2000, Australia
195 Broadway, New York, NY 10007, USA

Typeset in 10/12.5 Adobe Caslon Pro
By Saanvi Graphics Noida

Printed and bound at
Thomson Press (India) Ltd

'Om mani padme hum'

'With constant practice of mindfulness you can transform the impure body, speech and mind into the pure body, speech and mind of a Buddha.'

– Anonymous

Contents

CANCER - CHARIOT

LEO - STRENGTH

VIRGO - HERMIT

LIBRA - JUSTICE

SCORPIO - DEATH

SAGITTARIUS - TEMPERANCE

CAPRICORN - DEVIL

AQUARIUS - STAR

PISCES – MOON

Author's Note

This is my favourite section in the book because I get to write about things which are beyond predictions here. In fact, what I write in this section deals with the basis of existence. I will only discuss the importance of living in the moment, mindfulness and the adverse effects of mindlessness here. I have discussed anicca (impermanence) and apranahita (aimlessness) in previous books and will discuss another interesting concept or a theory associated with mindfulness in this book – the concept of 'No Mind'.

I first learnt about No Mind from the book *Zen Mind, Beginner's Mind*. What I love about this book is the way it presents the concept of No Mind. No Mind means a mind without the mind! Complicated isn't it? During the read, if you don't understand something or have questions, please feel free to drop me an email at karmel@tarotreader.in and I will be delighted to answer them.

Part I: What is No Mind?
Part II: Benefits of No Mind
Part III: Ways to achieve No Mind

Part I
What is No Mind?

I first heard about this concept in the film *The Last Samurai*. In the film, this concept is referred to as the basis of creation, the basis of the lives of the samurais. The film discusses how being in No Mind can actually help you achieve what you desire, and even help you attain salvation. Later I read up on this concept and discovered that No Mind means the space in your mind where your mind doesn't exist or is empty. This is the part of the mind which does not have ego, or the emotions of anger, desire, fear, love or hate. Can you imagine a time, even for a second, when you are free from the constant chattering in your mind? I am sure you have never experienced this state. But if you do think about this concept and do the work required, you may be able to glimpse the No Mind zone.

Whenever I can't sleep, I find I can hear my thoughts of fear and insecurity, pain and misery so loudly that they actually bother me. At times like this, I usually give up trying to sleep and simply give in to my chattering mind. This makes me the slave of my mind. You may be doing this too, when you are restless and unable to sleep. The mind is a formidable opponent. It is hard to defeat and will not go down without a fight.

The only way to train your mind to listen to you, to submit to you, is to create empty spaces in it; in other words, create a No Mind zone. No Mind is the state when thoughts don't exist, when you are open to everything, unlike in the normal state when your mind tends to latch on to thoughts and manipulates them. Let's try to understand how your mind behaves normally by looking at the example below:

Imagine you get a call from your boss and he tells you: 'Hey, listen, I want to talk to you about something important. This may not be such great news and I hope you take it well. Let me know when you are here and we can chat.'

While you are listening to this conversation, you may start having horrific thoughts, such as: 'Chat means what? Am I going to be fired? Oh God, yes I am going to be fired! No job means no money; I will default on my mortgage payment; I can't buy the car now; how will I pay my bills? My kid's school fees are not going to be paid! Oh God, I am doomed, I am a loser; What do I tell my wife/husband? What do I tell my friends? I will never find a job in time; it will take me a year to find a job that pays me this much! I am dead meat; I am doomed.'

These thoughts of anger, dejection and disappointment are all symptoms of a state which is just the opposite of No Mind. Observe how your mind drove you to assume what your boss was planning to say to you. You simply jumped to conclusions. You have no idea what your boss is going to discuss with you, but your mind has led you to focus on the worst-case scenario such as being fired! If you have had thoughts of this kind in other situations, then you know how you are enslaved to your mind and its incessant chattering.

Now if you were in the No Mind zone, you are likely to have handled the comment from your boss in the following way:

While you are listening to your boss talking, you will be fully present in the moment. You will be devoid of any prejudice, anger, resentment or thought. You will simply be listening. At the end of the call you will simply smile with amusement, wondering what your boss wants to discuss. You won't dissect the information he provided; neither will you judge it as good or bad. What the discussion will be about, what its outcome will be, doesn't concern you at all. You will put the phone down and resume what you were doing – maybe washing the dishes – before the call.

You will resume doing the dishes mindfully, and feel the water on your fingers and the foam of the liquid soap, and focus on rinsing the dishes. You will not reflect on the call you just received. You will simply be in the No Mind zone in which you are not attached to any thoughts, not disturbed by negative ideas; nor are you feeling joyous because of positive thoughts. This is how you are in a state of No Mind – when the mind is quiet and calm, focused on the task assigned to it.

Part II

Benefits of No Mind

You will benefit greatly when you achieve No Mind, even if it is for a second. Imagine a minute of no thought, no tension, no worries, no pain and no fear. Simply an empty mind! In such a state you can achieve eternal happiness. Unfortunately, the only people who seem to practise No Mind are the monks. If you speak to them, you will realize how detached they are from worldly desires, which makes them calm and peaceful.

You can begin to practise No Mind by taking small steps. Through this practice, you will achieve moments of bliss and learn to calmly handle the stressors in your life. No Mind teaches you to approach concepts in a detached manner, without any inhibitions and illusions. You simply look at everything from the perspective of a third person and are not affected by situations, problems or difficulties. You become the watcher, the observer who sees an emotion without identifying with it.

When you begin to observe your thoughts, you begin to exert control over your mind. You begin to drive your thoughts from a negative standpoint to a positive one. You begin to control your emotions. Whether you are feeling happy or sad, you will be aware of what is happening inside you. This gives you power over your mind. The next time you are in a difficult situation, start observing the mindless chatter in your mind and simply smile at it. As you begin to observe this noise in your head in a detached manner, your negative or positive emotions will disappear.

You could be involved in a situation where someone is screaming or pointing fingers at you. If you are in a state of No Mind, you will begin to look at this person as someone who is cursing your ego and trying to attach your mind. You will look at this person as someone who is wounded and needs to vent to feel better. You will begin to feel good that you could help this person because he/she could vent to you. You will begin to detach from your ego and, therefore, your mind.

Your mind will have control over you as long as your ego is involved. The moment the ego or I, me and mine disappears from your identity, your mind will no longer have power over you. You will then simply be in the present moment, where fears and inhibitions don't matter, where good and bad don't have any importance, neither does wealth. You become enlightened, and this realization – that you have power over your mind – becomes your greatest tool to achieve success.

If you start watching your thoughts and not identifying with them, you will achieve the following benefits:

- Anger and ego will lose their power over you. You will no longer have a bloated ego, nor will your tongue work faster than your thoughts. You will have control over both.
- Love, hatred, pain, misery and other emotions of this kind will have no impact on you.
- You will be calm in your approach and handle situations logically and practically.
- You will have greater clarity and your purpose will begin to surface.
- You will see beyond I, me and myself.
- You will be separated from yourself. You will become the watcher and will no longer be the thinker.
- You will have power over your feelings, emotions and thoughts.

The experience of No Mind will vary from person to person. You can judge its potential only after you begin to attain this state. To do that you need to learn how to achieve No Mind.

Part III

How to achieve No Mind

You cannot achieve a No Mind state overnight. It takes years and years of steady practice. Therefore, instead of attaining nirvana your focus should be on attaining a calm and composed demeanour so that you have positive thoughts and are able to channelize your energy into achieving a happy outcome. Everyone wants to be happy – new cars, a big home, a fat pay cheque, a hefty bank balance are all aimed at enhancing happiness. But happiness is actually a state of mind. It is the result of No Mind.

The following steps will help you align your mind towards No Mind:

1. Observe every thought; take note of your emotions

This is easier said than done. Your first reaction to any situation will be to identify with the situation and immediately get carried away by the chatter of the mind. Well this is the challenge – the moment such nonsensical blabbering begins in your head, stop and watch it like an external observer. If you do this often, you will begin to realize that when you observe a thought or a feeling, it loses its power over you. The more you tune in to your thoughts and feelings, the more easily you begin to detach yourself from them.

2. Walking, washing or driving meditation

Who says that meditation can only be done while you are sitting still in one place? Most people believe that meditation, is boring and slow. Instead of practising sitting meditation which is tough to do initially, you can practise something that comes more naturally to you; e.g., walking meditation.

You can do this when you are out for your daily walk. Simply watch every step you take. Observe how one leg goes up and the other stays down. Feel the pressure when your feet touch the ground. Count each step you take and name them – left down, right down, etc. This way you will be mindful while walking which will prevent your mind from wandering. If your mind does wander to the past or the future, gently bring it back to the present and begin counting each step again.

You can even try this approach while you are driving or washing dishes. Every time you are at the wheel, name every activity you perform while driving, such as accelerate, brake, etc. When your mind wanders, name it and gently bring it back to where it should be. Similarly, name what you do while washing dishes. This way your mind will gradually come under your control and you will know when it wanders.

3. Experiencing No Mind

After continuous practice of being the observer, you will begin to experience empty spaces. This may happen any time; for instance while you are having a cup of coffee. You may have no other thought in your mind at this time, except for the enjoyment of the coffee. You will be able to smell its aroma, taste its rich flavour and hear the gulping sound with every sip. This is when you will begin to notice the calm state of your mind, which is No Mind.

This state of mindfulness may not last longer than the time you take to drink the cup of coffee, but it will show you what true happiness feels like. You may also experience this state of No Mind when you are listening to a pleasant song. As you begin to enjoy this state of No Mind – when the mind is asleep but you are awake and alert – you will try to achieve it more often.

4. Books that can help you attain No Mind

I especially recommend the first two titles:

Zen Mind, Beginners Mind, by Shunryu Suzuki
An Introduction to Zen Buddhism, by D.T. Suzuki
Zen Doctrine of No Mind, by D.T. Suzuki
Zen: The Quantum Leap from Mind to No Mind, by Osho
Essays in Zen Buddhism, by D.T. Suzuki
Zen Buddhism and Psychoanalysis, by Erich Fromm, D.T. Suzuki, Richard De Martino
Mindfulness in Plain English, by Bhante Henepola Gunaratana
You are Here, by Thich Nhat Hanh
The Miracle of Mindfulness, by Thich Nhat Hanh
A Guide to Awareness, by Somdet Phra Nyanasamvara
Being Peace, by Thich Nhat Hanh
Be Free Where You Are, by Thich Nhat Hanh
Intuitive Awareness, by Ajahn Sumedho
The Diamond Sutra, by Osho
Dhamma Discourses on Vipassana Meditation, by Ven. Sayadaw Kundala

Becoming Your Own Therapist & Make Your Mind an Ocean, by Lama Thubten Yeshe
The Art of Living, by Ven. Master Chin Kung
Practical Insight Meditation, by Ven. Mahasi Sayadaw
Taming the Monkey Mind, by Cheng Wei-an
Cutting Through Spiritual Materialism, by Chogyam Trungpa
Lankavatara Sutra (Source – Buddhanet.net)

With this I end my journey with you this year.

ARIES

THE EMPEROR

Love Forecasts

January

There is likely to be a change for the good and you will yourself bring about this positive development. Your relationship will generally look very good at the start of the month but a little later you may develop some interpersonal problems and conflicts with your partner. You must speak up when needed and firmly hold your ground. The end of the month indicates a brief respite which will let your relationship breathe. This may be a solo break to get your thoughts and ideas straightened out, or you may take it with your beloved to rekindle the passion in your relationship. The single Aries will be busy planning the way forward to explore various options in love. The plan is clear – make yourself available but not look desperate. Be calm and act with poise to attract potential lovers.

February

You will be excited and eager to ring in the necessary changes to better your relationship. But when needed, do speak up and make yourself clear. I see you ending or putting a stop to something that you don't approve of in this relationship. An egalitarian approach will be most acceptable and will help the relationship. However, while you are working hard on establishing the right balance, do not be pushy, demanding or domineering. Avoid hasty decisions and desist from jumping to conclusions.

If you are single, then be ready to meet an interesting opposite who will sweep you off your feet.

March

I see you and your partner moving forward in establishing a healthy relationship. The situations around you will be positive and will serve to enhance your rapport. However, I see problems looming towards the end of the month when you are going to face difficulties and will have to watch where you are headed in love. The impulsive Aries who is single will meet someone interesting this month. Your hopes and desires with respect to love may soon be realized and you will find an eminently suitable partner.

April

I see that your love life is complete and fulfilling. You will feel rather poetic and may decide to use your creative skills to do something romantic for your beloved. At the end of the month, you will be blindsided by a change that may rattle this sweet castle of love that you have built. This turn of events is inevitable. There will be certain issues that you may face due to these unexpected developments and it's best to be fair to both yourself and your partner and to speak up when needed. Whatever is on your mind about this switchover, and where it can take your relationship, should be openly discussed to avoid future problems.

The single, childlike Aries will seek advice and guidance in matters of the heart from a responsible, respected and old-fashioned individual. If you listen to this person, you may strike gold.

May

The events that disrupted your love life last month will have some residual effects in May. You may find yourself feeling overwhelmed and tense due to your partner's lack of attention or a problematic situation that he/she may be in. It's best to stay put, stay supportive and continue to be as understanding as you can be. Despite your efforts, a little further into the month, these tensions will seem never-ending and you will find yourself beginning to lose patience and reacting rather than reciprocating. If you are unattached and looking for love, then May will bring forth someone romantic and kind-hearted. I see you wearing your heart on your sleeve, but you may want to be more practical and less romantic to see just where this infatuation goes.

June

I see you in a very good position in your love life in the early part of this month. Your partner will appreciate your support and all that you have done during the recent trying period, and this will only make your relationship sweeter. But as all good things come to an end, this peaceful interval will also draw to a close. I see conflicts, internal and external, arising in your romance. The end of the month will see you both growing in love and taking your relationship to the next level. You may decide to propose, or organize an event to formalize your relationship. For the singles who have decided to enter the fray to win the affection of a potential mate, beware of formidable rivals. On the upside, there is also a possibility that you may have more than one person vying for your love.

July

You are about to take the plunge and formalize your love affair, taking it to the next level. Middle of the month will bring forth happy times when you will manifest your greatest desire in love and you could get married or have a formal engagement. If you are already married, there will be new beginnings through positive developments in your love life. You and your partner will be in total harmony with each other. The single Aries will meet someone kind and generous this month, someone who could come forward through an acquaintance and bring a positive perspective to your life. However, you must evaluate this option thoroughly.

August

This will be a challenging month for your relationship. I see you calling it quits and ending what may have failed to work for you. This could be an arrangement that you may have made in other aspects of your life such as work, health or wealth. Although this call is going to be difficult to take, it is the sine qua non. You could also choose to relocate or move away from your partner to fulfil your passions and dreams. The end of the month looks positive when happiness will once again grace you. You will continue to be at peace and enjoy the stability as long as there is a balance in your relationship. You and your partner must strive to achieve this. The single Aries may feel left out when others look so happy with their beloved but all this is about to change. You just need to alter your attitude towards life and be positive.

September

You will have to stay put and be calm to see the results of your efforts. There is a strong likelihood that you will see the situation bear fruit in the near future; therefore, do not give up hope until then. Mid-month, you may face disappointments and be weighed down by the feeling that your partner underestimates your worth and isn't right for you. However, these conclusions may emerge from a heated discussion and a non-conducive environment. If you adopt a patient attitude and a calm demeanour, you are likely to see positive returns. Towards the end of the month, your relationship will take a complete 360-degree turn for the good. The single Aries needs to re-examine his/her own self-esteem and morale. How can you find true love when you don't truly appreciate who you are?

October

Either you or your partner will be busy toiling away at the workplace on a new assignment or a project. This is likely to take a toll on your love relationship because you or your partner will be too preoccupied to focus on love. Make time for love and do pay attention to the other's needs. During such trying times, especially with the recent imbalance in the relationship, you are likely to feel left out, cheated or disappointed due to the time constraints levied by the work overload. However, a much-needed change is in the offing and, towards the end of the month, I see you gradually moving towards stability. The single Aries should avoid acting out of desperation or going all out too aggressively. This is not the right time to manifest a good partner and it's best that you wait for the right opportunity.

November

A woman will play an important role in your love life this November. If she is someone you are attracted to outside your committed relationship, be forewarned about the risk you are taking. This is a magical phase of your love life and you may appear to be exceptionally attractive to others, which could also land you in trouble. Pay attention to your instincts and heed your intuition. You must learn to relinquish your idealized notion of a perfect relationship, to accept what you have in order to maintain peace and harmony in your existing love life. The last few days of the month will be a period of isolation which you can use to reflect on the way your relationship has panned out so far. You may be generally troubled due to other matters which may cause you to withdraw from your partner. It's good to take some time off to clear your mind but avoid ignoring your beloved.

If you are single, you can start this month to look for positive developments. I see you ready to move ahead and explore love. Your thoughts and ideas will bring forth what you seek.

December

There will be passion, attraction and romance between you and your partner in the beginning of December. Marriage or a formal engagement could be part of the plan and if you have been trying to conceive, then this is the month when that greatest wish could come true. I see you focused a lot on your work, but do not forget to dedicate time to your family and your beloved. Towards the last few days of the year, I see you at a crossroads with a momentous decision to make, but spoilt for choice and confused with so many options. This could be a key to other aspects of your life like health, wealth or career, but it may have a bearing on your love relationship as well. Choose wisely and carefully. The single Aries may find love this month. The long wait during the year will end pleasantly and I see you meeting and getting to know someone you already knew but never saw as a love interest.

Health Forecasts

January

In the first month of the year, you will be focused on repressing emotions which will eventually become a health issue. If you do not confront these issues and resolve them, they may just turn into ailments. A woman will play an important role in your life at this time. She could be pushy and headstrong. Know when to limit her influence. Sometime later in the month, I see a need to be practical and logical towards your body and mind. If you have been pushing yourself too hard, slow down, and if you have been slacking off, get disciplined. The end of the month shows happy times emotionally. You will have all that is needed to keep your heart happy and strong on a personal level.

February

You will see fruition of what you always wanted to health-wise, whether it is weight-loss, weight-gain, a certain fitness level or freedom from a particular illness. If you are expecting the results of a test, then know that the results will be good. You have done well and now the universe is signalling hope and positive outcomes. The end of the month will be an interesting phase when you may get a medical diagnosis that may rattle you a bit. If this isn't something you want to hear, then I would suggest that you go in for a second opinion.

March

This month, you may end a journey or association with something to move on, triggering a radical transformation on a spiritual level. The change is inevitable and the more open you are to it, the smoother the transition will be. Mid-month, you will begin to adapt to the new change and notice how wonderfully it is working for you. If there are still hints of distress, you should consider looking back in time, meaning your past, where you will find answers to your problems both at the physical and emotional levels.

April

You may have been pushing yourself too much and working too hard. You may want to ease off and take a breather because overdoing things will land you with health problems. Some news is on its way to you this month, although this may not be something you want to hear. However, be prepared, take the tidings stoically and work towards better health. I see your efforts coming to fruition. I see you triumphantly celebrating your success.

May

You will initiate a new routine, therapy or treatment that will help you achieve your desired health goals, although this may seem like an impossible feat right now. You will have to put your best foot forward, work hard and stay focused. If you slacken your pace, you will lose the momentum. There are others in the game who may seem to be making better progress. The end of the month will bring in some positive news. You will see progress because of your hard work, and this will only motivate you and keep you going to achieve greater results.

June

I see you making gradual but definite progress. However, overdoing anything will be detrimental to your health. Slow down, take it easy and relax to embrace the progress you have made. You will experience change in mid-June when you will have to end one activity or treatment and initiate another. This will be for your good and is essential at this juncture. You may never have experienced freedom the way you will now. You could take a break, a holiday, maybe even an international vacation to boost your confidence and make the most of your well-being.

July

Tensions and sadness greatly contribute to increased stress levels which can harm you. You must take care and ensure you keep these anxieties at bay. I see you feeling defeated, angry and cheated. Although you may want to be confrontational, it is best that you don't and keep calm instead. However, as this course could cause a dangerous eruption of repressed emotions, I suggest you vent your spleen by punching a pillow, screaming in a locked room or going for a long and tiring run. The end of the month will be better and you will decide to schedule some invaluable 'me time' and pamper yourself.

August

You may be caught between two opposing elements and a choice between the two may be impossible to make. There will also be some imbalance because of the tension caused by an incorrect choice. Know that it is crucial that equilibrium is restored. Eat right, sleep well, exercise regularly and meditate from time to time. Mid-month shows your health improving. You will feel alive and energetic and will choose to focus on the important facets of your life. But somehow the tendency to live in the past and regret what has gone by will revive the guilt and pain. Make it a point to live in the present and not in the past.

September

You will strive to strike the right balance between the various factors in your life. You may be worried about certain issues, and this anxiety could probably be about an ongoing health problem.

If something has been bothering you and your doctor is unable to diagnose it, it's best that you get to the bottom of it yourself and get a specialist's opinion. A medical practitioner will be a part of your health scene this month. His/her opinion will matter a lot and you will get clarity regarding the health issue. If you have been wondering about poor finances or insurance, then know that the universe will send you blessings and aid you in one way or another.

October

You will initiate a partnership with a new healer or a doctor who you believe can diagnose and treat your problem. This partnership will be positive and should produce favourable results. A change will occur this month which will upset the ease and comfort you have established so far. You will witness something remarkable in your health this month. Your outlook on life should improve and will be tinged with a new compassion. This is good considering how hard you have worked to establish such strong emotional stability. Keep it up!

November

Your emotional baggage from the past is debilitating to your health. It's time you let go of these memories. I see you on the road to recovery mid-month as you meet a strong and authoritative healer who is worthy of your trust. Towards the end of the month, I see you battling hypothetical problems. Stop identifying with these antics of your mind. Take control, relax and know that most of your worries are only imaginary, far from real.

December

A traditional healer or an institute which heals ailments in a traditional manner will play an important role in your life this month. It could be an Ayurveda expert or a spiritual healer. Although you may find the approach conservative, trust your instinct to stick with it, it will help you. You could also resort to visiting a counsellor who will adopt talk therapy and other such interventions.

All these methods will boost your mental and spiritual health which is exactly what you need at the end of the year.

You may realize that some of your issues can be resolved with answers from your past, especially your childhood memories. Or perhaps you bump into something or someone from the past who can become the key solution to your ongoing health problem. Keep your eyes and ears open for such developments. The last few days of this month will see you pushing yourself harder to achieve your desired health goals. My recommendation is: go slow!

Wealth Forecasts

January

If you have been thinking about spending money on home improvements and refurbishments, then hold on. Use your money prudently and avoid unnecessary expenditure. Very soon you will find what you have always desired with respect to money. There may be an unexpected windfall. A decision will have to be made and its best you use your intuition in this regard. If you are expecting a return on your investments or awaiting money which may have got stuck somewhere, and the delay seems protracted, the news will not be good. The money will come eventually but with further deferment.

February

You may face some anxiety regarding money this month. To be a millionaire, you need to have a millionaire's attitude. This attitude will develop when you share your money with the less fortunate. I see an acquaintance or a chance meeting with someone from your past who could open a gateway of opportunity for better prospects. The end of the month looks promising with news of money coming in. This good news will in turn lead to money-making opportunities which will generate wealth.

March

You will initiate something new with an intention to change the course of your finances. This could mean participating in a new venture or a start-up of some sort. Mid-month looks very positive and your wealth will show a steady increase. You may be tempted to spend a lot more than needed, but I don't advise that. Save for a rainy day and put your money to good use.

April

You may have to re-examine your expenditure and your money management. There seems to be a lack of balance. Be prudent and think before you leap. There will be a further delay in the returns, rewards or money you were expecting this month. You will definitely get your money but it will take time. Fortunately, the end of the month will be good for you, and your finances will be on an upswing. You will see some positive developments which may be small, but there will be progress for sure.

May

You are about to start something new such as a job or a part-time assignment which will give you more money. Someone, from somewhere, may just gift you money which will come in handy now. There will be complete balance in your finances with respect to your income and expenditure. You will be spending in important areas and putting the money to good use. After the imbalance witnessed last month, this positive news will certainly be welcome.

June

This month has mixed outcomes. It will start well with you continuing to maintain a balance in your life which will reflect positively on your wealth. There is equality and fairness in your spending and income. If you have the tendency to spend more than needed this month, stop and re-evaluate your finances. If you are eager to invest in a particular scheme, investigate it well and be sure about its returns. However, I would advise you against any investments this month. There is an arrangement that you may have to end which no longer yields the returns it did some time ago.

July

The cards that I see this month point to discipline, organization and balance. Reckless spending and an undisciplined attitude towards finances will land you in trouble. By mid-July, the situation will improve and your money flow will get better. You will be tempted to splurge, but try to curb this desire. At the end of the month, you will generally be feeling blessed about your current money scenario and will be content with the material assets you have acquired.

August

The situation doesn't look so good for you and your returns or rewards may seem less likely to come through. But worrying is not the solution to your problem. You could turn to a woman who could help you during this phase. She is kind and compassionate and will extend a helping hand by offering valuable advice and supporting you. You must feel gratitude for all that life has given you so far. The end of the month will remind you to review your income and outflow and tweak them to regain the balance. You may ink an important deal which will open a portal to greater wealth opportunities.

September

The initial part of the month could be challenging and I see you overwhelmed with financial burdens. There will be too much to do and too little money to manage all that you want to achieve. If you have been shying away from asking for help, then do not hesitate now. Mid-month will bring about a complete transformation in your financial well-being. All that you ever wanted will work out but it may not be in the manner that you planned. However, it will work out well for you and will help you recover from your financial slough.

October

Money has come to you with some difficulty and this has made you develop a tendency to hoard it. This attachment will become a problem. The more you worry about fiscal deficits, the more adversity you will attract. Instead, look at how you can give more to get more. You could consider looking at your past for some interesting openings or opportunities that can get you extra income. A walk down memory lane or a chance meeting with someone somewhere may just change the course of your actions. The end of the month will bring positive news of financial progress. You will get an unexpected offer or discover a new source of funds.

November

You may have to think twice this month before you plunge into a new scheme or financial plan. In my opinion, avoid investments entirely, but if you have to invest, thoroughly research it and opt for small investment schemes. You may come upon a sudden windfall a little further into the month. I do see you doing some charity work with good intent. This will go into your good karma. The end of the month will mark your recovery where your finances will begin to look up and stability will be established. But do not give in to the temptation to splurge.

December

You will have a good start to the last month of the year. I see you spending money on giving yourself a much-overdue pampering. There is enough to save and some to spend. Mid-month, you may witness a life-transforming event which will disrupt the financial balance that you have established. This incident could be related to your job, to falling stocks, crumbling investments and real estate hitting an all-time low. You will do phenomenally well as soon as you come to terms with this difficult change, which may seem devastating at first. At the end of the month, I see you achieving closure of some sort which will promise wealth and prosperity in the year to come. You will be back with a bang and will have overcome the upsetting change and walked the path of renewal. This is how the year will end for you financially.

Career Forecasts

January

The year will start very well with a woman playing an important role in your career. With her guidance and support you can initiate the new beginnings which have been waiting in the wings. New and positive developments are about to take place this month. If you were expecting a certain position, a job offer or a role change, it will be on its way to you. The end of the month will see you in a new and challenging role, and you will learn the ropes and the nature of the work from scratch. Although this role may be new territory, you will have the intention to acquire all the knowledge you need to prove yourself to succeed in this position.

February

I see you stressed and tense about the work and how you are perceived in this new set-up. The nagging suspicion that you are being excluded will tend to raise your hackles, but you must control your temper and ego and remain calm. I see the situation improving for you in the middle of the month. You will begin to receive positive reactions, accolades and recognition for your work. An international holiday or an overseas assignment may come your way. Make the most of this opportunity. You have worked very hard and I see you approaching the finish line towards the end of the month. Now is the time to tie up the loose ends and complete what you have started.

March

You may be pushing too hard or thinking in a negative direction right now. Take some time off to redirect your thoughts on a positive path. If you lack the patience to stay in this present position, it may be time to scout for a change. If you are seeking a job, then this month end will bring in some good news in the form of offers and new opportunities. In your existing set-up, the situation will begin to improve and you will glimpse a silver lining.

April

You will be at the top of your game where everything will be moving in the right direction for you. You will undertake extensive domestic air travel for your work. You may also be involved in a partnership with another individual during this time. An overseas opportunity may be on your mind as well, and this may come through. However, the end of the month poses some challenges. You may let your ego come in the way and feel cheated or disappointed about something or someone. This will cause temporary hurt but you will recover provided you don't pay too much heed to it.

May

Your work will look very good with mostly positive outcomes at the beginning of the month. Although this month starts well, you will soon enter a phase when you may have to juggle between two important aspects of your career. Towards the end of the month, something may go dreadfully wrong and you may need to take the call to end what is not working out and move on. This may be an uncomfortable decision but it is needed. If you are looking for a job, then be informed that the opportunity that you pinned your hopes upon may not work out, leaving you feeling dejected.

June

You will face stiff competition from formidable opponents, so put your best foot forward, play fair and see what comes your way. Do not bother about those who play deceitfully. Victory will come only from playing fair. I see you in a celebratory mood mid-month when there could be parties or events lined up. A partnership of three people may be on the cards. This will be short-lived but definitely fruitful. Towards the end of the month, a woman will play an important role in your life. She will be headstrong and talented and if she collaborates with you, she will point you in the right direction.

July

You may choose to leave a situation that may not be working out for you. This will be a difficult decision but it must be made considering the odds that you are facing. July is also the time when you may have to re-evaluate your options to see if there is anything you can do to enhance the way you work. An alternative may be offered to you which may seem unfair at first, but from where I see it, if you accept this change and improve yourself, the rewards will flow in. The end of the month is when I see you triumph, overcoming all hurdles to win accolades and the confidence of your peers.

August

There may be some inequity at your workplace. You will have to watch your back, beware of people who seem nosy and interfering, and watch out for situations where your seniors or colleagues may steal your credit. The best way to deal with this difficulty, which will pass eventually, is to stay calm and be vigilant. Towards the end, a nostalgic period may influence your work positively. There may be something or someone from the past who will play an important role in your workplace and bring you some happiness, even if it's temporary. A walk down memory lane may help you revitalize.

September

A positive partnership is on the cards. There is a woman who is smart and witty, who could be a senior, subordinate or a colleague and has the power to influence your performance. If you could liaison with her you will benefit greatly. But otherwise keep her at bay as she could pose a potential threat in the future. If you begin to adopt a more compassionate and appreciative outlook towards your job, you will be able to make peace with what you have and attain a marked improvement in your productivity.

October

You may start a new assignment or job this month. This will be a challenging, exciting and rewarding time. However, a little further into the month, the work pressures may start building up and you will find yourself getting annoyed with the endless challenges and the people around you. You could feel cornered and defeated. The end of the month will see you in a happy zone, embracing freedom and loving every bit of your work. You will be jubilant having come out with flying colours against all odds. You may have decided to take a short break, either international or domestic, which will give you some space to breathe, relax and plan your way forward with more clarity.

November

You may have mixed feelings about other people. It's best, under such circumstances, to watch what you say. Handle people with kid gloves, especially those who have the tendency to discredit you or put you down. This month will be similar to September. Be patient and the situation will turn in your favour. Help and motivation will come from memories, people or things related to your past. A chance acquaintance may just bring forth an opportunity that could help you deal with your current circumstances.

December

You may decide to leave your existing set-up if you are dissatisfied with it. However, if you are going to continue in your current workplace, then know that the situation is about to change and will favour you. I see you poised on the brink of a lot of action, and you will be busy strategizing and planning the way ahead. A woman will be very supportive in this task and will help you with your larger goal. The end of the month will bring forth your greatest dream or passion related to your ambition. If there is one thing that you have truly wished for from your work – it will come to life at this juncture.

TAURUS

THE HIEROPHANT

Love Forecasts

January

It's the start of the year and a good time to communicate clearly with your beloved. If the communication fails, all else will too. You may be unhappy about several aspects of your relationship but unless you speak up how will your partner understand what you want. Further into the month, I see conflicts arising between you and your partner. You will be anxious and worried about this relationship and you may even consider giving it all up and taking the easy way out. But hang on; after coming so far, you could wait and watch because the situation may improve if you give it some time.

The single Taurus will be spoilt for choice. You may have more than one option to explore in love. But don't be hasty with your decisions. Make your choice with wisdom and tranquillity.

February

Difficulties lie ahead and these are going to make it impossible for your relationship to have a happy ending. By now you may be certain that this relationship may not work out for you and are looking for closure. I see that you have realized after deep reflection that there is very little you can do but accept this negative situation. Sometime later in the month you may find yourself moving too quickly to work things out, or your partner could be pushing you to do so. You may feel pressured to stay in a relationship that you know isn't right. Use your judgement and know when to assert yourself. You must do what you feel is right. You or your partner must learn to let go and avoid being clingy. If something is truly yours, it will return to you, let it go. But pushing your choices and weaknesses on others isn't a good approach at this point.

If you are unattached, then this February you may be poised on the brink of a transformation which will lead you to your potential lover.

March

This month is crucial for your love life. I see that you will have many options to make a romantic choice or make a decision that will impact your love life. Look before you leap and think through your decision calmly. If you are in this relationship for the sake of comfort or because of fear or insecurity of some kind, then it's high time you stopped fooling yourself and ended what may not be working for you. The end of the month is a good time for love as you will feel more attractive and will be ready to fall in love once again.

The single Taurus needs to make time for love between your working career and other aspects of life. Otherwise you will simply be delaying your prospects for love.

April

If you are in a relationship that makes you feel restricted and constrained, it's time to speak firmly and clearly. You have the power to change the situation if you should so desire. A woman, someone senior, will steamroll you into accepting her opinions and ideas about a love relationship. You need to limit her influence to the extent that is useful for your current relationship. The end of the month is a time to look at life more emotionally and compassionately. I see that you will adopt an approachable attitude and become more open to your partner's ideas and thoughts.

If you are seeking love, then you could get attracted to someone much older. Do not rule out this person due to his/her age as there could be potential for a healthy love relationship.

May

You could be considering an official announcement of your commitment through formal events within the family. While this decision will leave you and everyone around you happy, do remember to give yourself and your partner some space from time to time. Being clingy may ruin everything. Understand that love grows when you respect each other's space and give each other a break from time to time. The end of the month will bring forth a conflict which will arise due to lack of space or freedom either for you or your partner.

The single Taurus will be seen strategizing and making plans to find love. Avoid desperation entirely.

June

You may be stuck in a relationship that you know has no future. You may have done everything in your capacity to work things out but sadly your relationship may see a harsh end. You may be at a point where difficult decisions will have to be made. The end of the month may present another delicate situation where matters are likely to get heated very easily. You will have to handle the situation calmly and avoid confrontations to whatever extent needed. If you are involved in a clandestine love affair, then know it will come to an end.

The unattached Taurus is in for some good news on matters of the heart. You will receive a message that will open a portal to explore opportunities in love.

July

I see you giving your best and in return receiving what you deserve from your partner in love. A relationship where there is mutual give and take will only grow. If it is financial aid that you have to give or receive, be open to it. Middle of the month will bring forth happy times where I see your love for each other scaling new heights. There will be further positive developments in your love life around the end of the month. You may seem more attractive than ever before to your partner and this will give you the confidence and faith to move forward in your love life.

The unattached may have to accept a sudden change which will eventually bring all the good you desire, especially in matters of the heart.

August

This month is simply fabulous for your love life. I see you steaming ahead in a relationship that has balance, harmony, and mutual love and respect. You may take your relationship to the next level and consider an official engagement or marriage, where families could be involved and happiness lies ahead for all those who are a part of your life. The end of the month ushers in a good omen. You will be feeling on top of the world and completely, truly, madly and deeply in love.

The single Taurus needs to pay attention to his or her life in general. Are you truly ready to fall in love? If so, are you making arrangements and working towards them? Reflect upon this!

September

You may find yourself dithering about making a momentous decision in matters of the heart because of the various choices before you. This decision is going to greatly influence your love life, hence choose wisely and carefully. I can see a change coming your way which will shake up all that you have created in love so far, but you will have no choice but to accept what comes next. The end of the month will see you in a difficult situation where you will be unable to strike a balance. You may be battling between two important aspects of your life, and your love life may take a hit.

If you are unattached, then this month will present an interesting situation where there may be more than one option for potential lovers. Choose wisely, without haste.

October

You have reached a phase this October where your love life may be losing its lustre. There is a quantum of boredom that may be troubling you, and you may be questioning all the good in your life. Perhaps you are pinning your hopes on your partner and he/she isn't able to fulfil all your expectations. The good news is I see your relationship sailing through this phase and maturing in love and rising to a new level of commitment and understanding.

The unattached Taurus will be too busy with unresolved emotional baggage, which will make love impossible. Try to fix it before you are ready to explore love.

November

There is a need to get more organized and practical about your approach in love. If you are being too laid back and complacent, your love life will be affected. Taking each other for granted and losing focus in love will only harm the relationship. An older person is part of your love scene this month. I see you receiving a message of love. This will uplift you emotionally as happy times are here again.

In case you are single and seeking love, then correct your expectations and be realistic. Do not pin your hopes on others as this will disappoint you.

December

The year will end on a positive note for your love life. There will be a strong bond of love between you and your partner, which will override most differences. Around mid-month, you will need to adapt to the changes that life throws at you and you will also have to make positive changes in yourself for the greater good of the relationship. You may have to swallow your ego, take a step back and be more accommodating to continue to maintain the peace. The last few days of the month will see you in complete control of your vision and goals in love.

The single Taurus will get what he or she desires in love. Your long wait for love ends here as you manifest your dream lover this December.

Health Forecasts

January

The year starts with a message. In all probability this news may relate to an ongoing health issue or it may bring to light something new altogether. If you are expecting health test reports, then be aware that the news may not be so good. If you feel a second opinion may put your doubts to rest, then go and get it. Emotionally there is a deep disconnect within you. If you have repressed emotions then it's time to deal with it. You should consider help and perhaps talk to a therapist or a healer. The end of the month, however, will usher in happy times. You may decide to take a break and relax.

February

February starts well. A sudden chance meeting with someone from the past may rekindle good memories. You will momentarily find solace and happiness in those happy times. If you have been facing problems of repressed emotions, then you could consider looking back at your childhood memories because the solutions to your troubles lie there. A little further into the month and pointless regret about situations and events from the past, which were never in your control in the first place, will start preying on you. This kind of brooding will manifest on a physical plane. The month ends with you being involved in a happy celebration and parties.

March

This month I see you struggling to cope with an unexpected and sudden revelation. Instead of worrying about it, I would suggest that you take control and find ways and means to deal with this problem. Middle of the month shows a phase where a change may come along and help you deal with your health issues. You should consider taking a break from everything and reflect upon your health peacefully. The end of the month will be a time for discipline and an organized approach. You cannot take your body for granted and cannot have irrational goals. Plan to bring some discipline into your lifestyle – eat right, exercise as needed and rest when it is time.

April

There is a need to consider the treatment of a good doctor or a healer who shall manifest this April. The healer will be effective in healing you and finding solutions to your problem. But if you have any doubts about your health, you should consider another opinion. If you are under the influence of drugs or are into substance abuse, then this phase indicates a very strong tendency to overindulge. This will land you in a mess from which a return may seem impossible.

April is also a time to watch your mental health. If you have a tendency to have emotional outbursts, then it's time to visit a clinical psychiatrist who could help you with the right medication. Do not hesitate to ask for help and be open to addressing your issues.

May

You could be gearing up for a change which will set the course for positive developments. Discipline, logic and hard work are going to be your weapons in dealing with your issues in the future. Please ensure you have a disciplined lifestyle with the right balance in eating, resting and playing. You cannot be lethargic and you definitely cannot take your health for granted. A healer or a doctor may come along and restore your health and help achieve good results.

June

Love and compassion can heal the worst of ailments. This love and compassion, if pointed inwards, can help ameliorate most of your chronic health problems. You must adopt a gentle approach towards yourself; don't be harsh and pushy. Instead learn to respect your body, mind and soul. A well-balanced life with a balance between your personal and professional life will go a long way in managing your stress. If there is gnawing resentment growing within you, vent your feelings in ways which help you. Do not hurt or ignore your body in any way now.

July

You could be battling some serious health problems and this could make you feel very run down. In fact, your efforts so far may prove futile and the ailment will seem to be gaining ground. You must take care and do everything possible to minimize the risks. Ensure that medical care is within your reach. Emotionally as well, this month will be challenging. If you have a tendency to overdo anything, then curb it right now. This includes overworking, overexerting or worrying too much. You will become a slave of your negative approach towards your body. You need to know your body's limits and to what extent you can make it work for you. The end of the month will be more difficult. I see you struggling with worries, feelings of disappointment and distrust. Other factors of your life may contribute to this phase which will suppress you emotionally.

August

After a difficult patch, you will get some respite and feel a sense of achievement this month. It may feel like a completion after working so hard to achieve your goal for your well-being. You may have accomplished the targets for your weight-loss or such other fitness goals. This may also mean a time where you may have finally overcome a chronic medical condition.

September

If you have been seeking a certain treatment, financial aid to back this treatment or a doctor or healer who can treat you, your efforts will finally bear fruit. You will see your greatest wish with regard to health become a reality. A woman who is not to be trifled with is part of your health scene this month. She will set some mandates and targets that you will have to follow and she will do what is best for your health. However, be assertive and say no when you feel your body can no longer take it. The end of the month is a fabulous time for you emotionally. I see you spending time with your family and loved ones when your health will look at its best and you will have a million reasons to be grateful to the universe.

October

You will begin a new journey this month, and do something new which will help improve your health. This may be a yoga class, a gym, a certain diet or a therapy or treatment which promises better health and success. I am glad you are taking up new initiatives as the rewards will be huge if you do make it to the other side. Go for it!

But not too long into this adventurous initiative and you may begin to feel compromised and tied down. The challenge may be too much for you, entailing sacrifices that you are unwilling to make. However, if you make it through this regimen, you will know that you have established a new level of fitness and made a complete recovery.

November

Certain tried and tested remedies may have been lost in the mists of time. I see a certain memory, person or something that emerges from your past reopening long-forgotten chapters. This flashback is in a way good as it may show you the way forward. You will achieve completion and attain success in the goals that you have assigned to your body and mind. You will complete what you started some time ago. Emotionally too, you are going to be stable and quite calm. I see that some positive news regarding your health is on its way to you.

December

The most important thing that you will walk away with this year is the idea of loving yourself and giving yourself due credit. If you are someone who lives for others, then it's high time you paid attention to your own needs first. There will be perfect balance and harmony towards the end of the year. I see you doing things in the right quantity and proportion which is what your health demands. However, in the last few days, you may binge and upset this exquisite equilibrium. Do not overdo or underperform any task that has been instrumental in benefitting your health.

This concludes your health predictions and I move on to your wealth forecasts in 2018. Wealth is another important aspect of your life and plays a vital role in your mental serenity.

Wealth Forecasts

January

The year opens with a sudden twist and an unexpected series of events that will bring an influx of income for you this January. The money should make up most of your deficit. However, there is a need to budget your spending and ensure there isn't any unnecessary extravagance. If the splurge is unavoidable, try to stagger your spending over a period of time. You will be in a good position towards the end of the month when you may consider starting something new. Your finances look promising and opportunities will come your way to bring in more wealth.

February

You are to set off on an adventure and journey into the unknown with an initiative which is likely to be both promising and risky. This may mean an investment opportunity or a venture which looks promising. You will do well this month as your money will grow and may even double or triple. However, do look out for the changes this venture could entail. You may feel confined or in a situation of compromise. Nevertheless, beyond this sacrifice lies redemption and its rewards will more than offset your concession.

March

Jubilation lies ahead. You will have enough money to spend and, more importantly, you will also be able to set aside something for a rainy day. Your efforts will pay off and you reap the rewards for all your hard work. Nevertheless, do look out for the last few days of the month when your financial situation may get a little tight. If this does happen, then prioritize your expenses to ensure the important ones are met first. This financial low is temporary and will change before you know it.

April

You are about to receive some good news. If you were pondering on a way to change your source of income, then this news may set the course for such a change. When everything seems to be going well, your mind may begin to turn negative with thoughts of insecurity and fear. Don't be restricted and locked away in such pessimism. However, the end of the month will be a fabulous time when all your wishes will be fulfilled. If you had a specific financial goal, you will achieve it at the end of April.

May

There could be a theft or breach of trust of some sort which will cause you some financial loss. Stay away from unscrupulous characters, and do thorough research before you invest money. You may have to stay calm and avoid jumping to conclusions or making hasty decisions. But nothing in life is constant, and this phase will soon pass. Good times will be here again and you will move away from all the deficits you suffered at the beginning of the month.

June

Your finances will look positive and be on an upswing as you step into June. Nevertheless, it is imperative that you apply logic and research before you opt for an investment avenue, and heed your head, not the sentiments of your heart. I see that you will receive a hefty windfall. You may consider reinvesting this money back into your business or think of starting a new line. You will undertake a journey at the end of the month. You are about to set foot into untested territory where both the risks and the stakes are high.

July

This month, the balance sheet will be lopsided with too much expenditure and too little revenue. There is nothing wrong in asking for help when needed, and it can bring in some respite. A little further into the month, your situation will improve. You may consider buying a vehicle or tickets to go on a vacation. While you must fulfil your wishes, you should first repay any debts you have. The end of the month may present a tough time once again when you may have to compromise a bit to ensure smooth financial sailing.

August

You will be gung ho to take on new initiatives and move forward to achieve your financial goals. But once again I see the card of deceit or theft. You should watch your back with people who make unrealistic promises and may siphon away your money. Do not put your money away in a place where it is not backed by thorough research and careful consideration. The end of the month will bring forth an opportunity that will emerge from your past. You will come upon a memory, a person or something that can open a doorway to an alternative source of income.

September

You may consider evaluating new financial avenues that give you confidence. You will be eager to launch into these avenues but ensure that you have researched them well. This month will generally be very positive and I see you getting lucky with money. This money will flow in from unexpected sources like a lottery, from forgotten ancestral income or from a gamble. There is a person who is senior in age and experience whose ideas and guidance will come in handy around the end of this month. He is someone who has sound knowledge about investments and I see him counselling you and steering you in the right direction.

October

Your finances will hit an all-time low due to a sudden revelation that will bring your dream castle tumbling down. This event will tarnish all that you have created so far and leave you devastated and weak. Fortunately, you will begin to recoup mid-month. Your work will swiftly pick up pace and this will account for a major part of your income. A very important feature of your finances will come into play this month and work wonders for you. You will once again see hope and better prospects will seem to be a reality, albeit a distant one.

November

Look before you leap this month. If you are planning to make an important financial or business decision then be absolutely clear about it. In my opinion, back it up with thorough research and conviction. This period is likely to be a little risky, hence avoid any immediate and hasty decisions. A positive change will be coming your way. This change will occur because of the karmic good that you have done in a past life. The end of the month indicates a time of discipline and rationale. I see this card in your reading regularly which makes me believe that you have the tendency to splurge. Be pragmatic and adopt a practical approach in managing your finances. Spend only as much as you need to, avoid miscalculated investments and overspending and repay your debts first.

December

You will receive an unexpected bonus for your efforts. You should use this money logically and perhaps reinvest it in a growing business. It is quite possible that you may consider starting a business of your own and the timing couldn't be more conducive than now. As you approach the end of the year, your finances will once again start looking up. You have been working towards something important financially and this will be achieved this December. I see good things coming to you as you bid adieu to the year and get ready to start a new one.

Career Forecasts

January

The year will start well, with you being in complete control of your career and your goals. However, if you have been expecting news related to a job offer, a new assignment or any other work, this is likely to get delayed further. Stay focused and, more importantly, stay positive. The end of the month will see you starting up a new initiative. You may decide to launch a business, take up something new alongside a job or simply start an alternate career. You have all that it takes to make this dream work.

February

This month is going to be exceptional for your career. I see you at the top of your game, with prosperity and success close at hand. You will do quite well in your job and I see money coming in a big way in the form of rewards and recognition. There is a big break coming your way which will fulfil a dream you have always had for your career. This opportunity may be a job, role or promotion which you have been expecting and working on.

But do look out for the end of the month as I see you being too pushy and tough on others. This approach may land you in trouble; so it's best to tone it down a bit to achieve your targets and goals.

March

You should take some time off and reflect on your past, seeking answers to all your questions regarding your career difficulties.

Your past may hold a solution either by bringing forth a memory, a contact, or something which can help you resolve your worries. If you are awaiting a job offer or a career change, then it's likely to come through this month. While you are poised on the brink of action, ignore those who are discouraging and stay away from office gossip and politics.

April

Your career is on an upswing and there will be positive developments which will move you forward. The progress on your work may be gradual but it will move you up in your career graph. You will be seen initiating new plans and executing work to achieve your final outcome. You may also undertake land travel within a specified region to meet your work requirements. However, do look out for the end of the month when deceit or distrust is likely to surface. Someone somewhere may cheat you or lie to you, breaking their commitment to you.

May

You will be in for some good news this May if you have been expecting a raise, promotion or a job change. I see your desires and hard work coming to fruition. The rewards will be big and you most certainly deserve them. This month a mentor or a teacher may step in. This mentor's guidance will be crucial and will help you greatly in establishing a sound career path. Do not try to change the old traditional norms, instead adapt to them. Rather than changing the situation outside, bring about a change within.

June

If you feel bogged down in a set-up which does not recognize or reward you, then you should change this instead of succumbing to the security and stability this kind of job offers. You need to look within and ask yourself whether the work makes you happy and you are feeling appreciated and valued. Mid-June you may feel shattered about a broken promise. The end of the month will be a harbinger of some positive news of a job change or an offer which will leave you happy and motivated.

July

July will be another positive month for your career. I see you doing very well in your work where most of your concerns will be resolved, and you will outshine others with your performance and capabilities. I see you receiving rewards for your contribution in terms of money incentives, bonus or a promotion. Avoid stepping into others' shoes and keep your temper at bay. It's best to handle difficult situations calmly and patiently. There could be some news coming your way which may not sound so positive, but will be news you could use.

August

You will channelize your energy in the right direction and put it to good use to achieve the outcome that you so desire in your career. A sudden change will shake the very foundation of your career which seems to be so strong. This change is inevitable and mighty, and there is nothing you can do to stop it or avoid it. All that is in your power is to adapt to it and move on.

September

There is positive news coming your way and this should boost your career. However, there could be conflicts arising at the workplace with your seniors and colleagues. You may witness a situation where you could feel disregarded despite your contributions. In my opinion, you should just stay calm and not pick on anyone right now. Despite all these tensions, the month will end well with a casual reunion, an office party or a celebration for a partnership deal inked between three partners.

October

The problems that you faced in the middle of last month will begin to settle down this month. A man who is senior and compassionate will step into your work scene this month. His guidance will help you build your career and easily achieve your goals. This is also the time when you should look at your job with gratitude, love and respect. The end of this month won't be so good and I see you feeling neglected when it comes to work opportunities and prospects for growth. Your job could go through a rocky phase during the last few days of this month; so be prepared.

November

Your work pressure is going to be at an all-time high this month, overwhelming you completely. If you manage to complete all the tasks assigned to you, do remember to take some time off and rest. I see you moving away or relocating in order to fulfil your career passion. Whatever you may have done until now didn't quite work out the way you wanted it to and you may have made up your mind to end this association and move on in pursuit of happiness and success. This decision is good and will open up avenues for better things.

December

You will initiate a new project or job this month which promises greater wealth prospects and happiness. However, do look out for a change that may come along. This will be more like a compromise, or let's call it a sacrifice, that you will have to accept or make initially for your greater good. The last few days of this month will find you in a quandary where you may feel constrained and held back due to some recent developments. You may not be in a position to speak your mind or you may feel hesitant and fearful to do so. Nevertheless, in my opinion, you should simply break free from these internal limitations that you have placed on yourself and do what you think is right.

GEMINI

THE LOVERS

Love Forecasts

January

If you are committed to someone, there may be certain differences and conflicts that will need your attention. You will need to hold your ground because not everything is fair in love. You may have to speak up and make yourself heard. Your relationship will reach a happier stage mid-month when I see mutual give and take. You and your partner will be sharing love, respect and kindness as well as financial aid. The end of the month will be a time when your efforts will pay off. You will be appreciated for what you have done and for the kind of person you are.

The single Gemini will be eager to start the hunt for a wise and true lover. This search will be coupled with excitement and eagerness to fall in love, and the readiness to attract what you want.

February

You will be in a space where your partner will be more approachable and more willing to share than usual. There is compassion and love in this relationship. Both of you will mature in love this month and reach a new platform of stability, trust and confidence in each other. The end of the month will be a magical time, when your relationship will be all set for a new beginning. Both you and your partner will be getting ready for something big which will take your love life to the next level.

The unattached Gemini may get invited to a marriage ceremony, an engagement party or some other important event of this kind where meeting a prospective lover will be a distinct possibility.

March

If you are stuck in a relationship that feels more like bondage, then it's time you break free from its shackles. Nonetheless, I see you willingly accepting the thraldom of this relationship which you know very well isn't going anywhere. Despite all this, the good news is that the one you love also cares for you and is willing to work on this relationship. Perhaps the approach adopted by your partner was wrong but he/she is willing to change and do the needful to mend fences. The end of the month will be a time of love and understanding, and also a time when both of you will be willing to work on your relationship.

The Gemini seeking love will have to contend with formidable rivalry in pursuit of a love interest. On the flip side you may have a wide array of suitors to choose from.

April

You are about to initiate a new beginning in your love life and I see you excited and eager about this. You and your partner now share a strong bond of love and are ready to explore greater possibilities in your relationship. When everything is going well, your mind will play its games. You may begin to feel insecure and fearful about this relationship, wondering if it will last forever. It is always advisable to speak your mind to your partner when there is doubt and suspicion, instead of living with these negative emotions.

If you are looking for love, then you need not look too far. A person who is already part of your life may be interested in you. You should consider giving this person a fair shot at love.

May

Your love life in general will be going well and I see reasons to celebrate and share your love with those around you. The celebration could be initiated for your anniversary or a birthday party planned by your partner. This mid-month will be a time for love, and there will be happiness, peace and love in your relationship. However, look out for the end of the month when trust issues will play a crucial role. One partner will not be completely honest with the other. If this is so and if you have this nagging feeling that something is off somewhere, bring it up and discuss it before the issue snowballs into something worse.

The single Gemini has every reason to be happy. You will see victory in love, and you will win the heart of the person you have always desired.

June

You and your partner may decide to call it quits this June. Although this will be a harsh decision, it's important that you take it. There is love beyond this phase as I see a man who will help you out and be your guide. The end of the month will be a magical period when you may have to use your intuition to guide you out of the situation you are in. An inner voice will show you the way. A woman may be involved in your love scene. If you are a male Gemini, then know that she is beyond your reach.

The single Gemini has a lot to look forward to this month. A loving person, who could be the right fit for you, is headed your way. You should get ready for the adventure that lies ahead.

July

There's a new development around the corner. This will make your life very exciting and intriguing, obviously rubbing off on your love life. Both you and your partner are in need of space and a break. This may mean a vacation together where you are exploring new places and having adventures hand in hand, or it may mean that this is not the time to be whiny or clingy but rather give each other some well-deserved space and make your own individual travel plans. I see you taking control of your life and strategizing plans to meet your desired goals.

If you are single and wondering why a relationship is not working out for you, it's time you wrought some important changes in yourself. You may have to look within to understand which areas you need to address in order to allow love into your life.

August

I see a truth surfacing suddenly which is going to torpedo your castle of love. This reality has been festering for some time. You may have to revise your approach towards love and life in general to keep the peace. These changes will not be easy to adapt to but it is imperative that you do so. The going will get tougher towards the end of the month when I see you questioning your love life. However, before you judge your partner's contribution, I suggest you do some introspection and examine your input in this relationship.

If you are unattached and seeking love, there is a possibility of a further delay. Things are not going to fall in place as anticipated.

September

A change is due this month which will disrupt the peace you had in love. This turn of events could emerge from your love life or other aspects of your life. However, all that you can do is to make a few compromises and adapt to the situation. It is crucial that you do so in the larger interest of your love life. Soon, a good omen will arrive which will herald an amelioration in your relationship. Both you and your partner will experience the other's compassionate side, and feel your love and respect grow stronger.

The single Gemini will have to juggle two important aspects of life to make time for love. You should consider balancing your work with personal life before it's too late to get to where you want to be in love.

October

You may be wont to jump to conclusions and take hasty decisions about your lover this month. However, hold your horses and think before you leap. This period isn't right for impetuous judgements.

The past will play an important role in driving you to behave like this. Are you holding on to your past or your partner's? If so, then it's high time to let go. However, if you feel there is an imbalance in this relationship and you find yourself being nose-led, it's time to speak up. Do what makes you happy and take control of the situation.

The unattached Gemini will have to shift his/her focus away from work and into love. All work and no play will make you dull, and love will not come to you in this way.

November

This month there will be bickering in your love life. It is always advisable to be in an egalitarian relationship in which both you and your partner have freedom of expression. Good news could be winging its way to you. This message could be coming from other areas of your life but it will uplift you and put both you and your partner in a happier zone. The end of the month sees your relationship maturing with both of you in total harmony with each other.

If you are single, then get ready for new beginnings in love this November. The situation is likely to change and get a whole lot better to favour you in your search for true love.

December

If you wanted a commitment, a marriage or a relationship which is complete, then you will have it all now. This is the beauty of this month. You will be moving into a phase in your life when most of your worries, insecurities and inhibitions revolving around your love life will be allayed. You will be more at ease with your partner, as though both of you have reached a certain stability after all the squabbling. The last week of the year will see your wish come true in love. This will uplift you emotionally and spiritually, leaving you happy and content. What an incredible year it has been for you in love!

The single Gemini may take a beating this month with all your plans failing to attract love to you. However, this defeat is temporary and the situation will change, as change is the only constant in life.

Health Forecasts

January

The year will start positively with your health getting better than before. If you are suffering from a particular ailment, you could consider changing your physician or a change of scene to refresh you and generate some clarity. I see you emotionally happy and geared up to take on the new year with zeal and zest. This positive attitude is good and it will help you manifest one of your greatest wishes in health. If you have been yearning for something related to health, that desire may soon materialize. The end of the month sees you initiating a partnership with a healer, a new doctor or a therapist who will help you manage your health better.

February

You will be on the brink of initiating a new health regimen which promises greater benefits. Balance is the key to success in your present physical condition. Take a moment to assess whether you are balancing your work and personal life well, as well as your diet and exercise routines. These are some of the areas where balance can play an important role. You will have to ensure moderation where needed. The end of the month will see a headstrong woman entering your health scene. She could be a person who is personally close to you or may be a healer or a doctor. Her influence will be good as long as you know where to draw the line.

March

An autocratic man will play an important role in your health this month. He will chart out plans and routines to which you will have to strictly adhere. This person could be a health practitioner or an instructor of some sort who has a rough edge when it comes to people management skills. You will benefit greatly if you do as he suggests. An important event or achievement is due this month. You will be manifesting a long overdue health goal, maybe weight-loss, weight-gain or a certain fitness level, this month.

April

You reap the fruits of your labour this month. If you have been exercising to achieve a certain goal, you will be successful. You will generally be happy with your achievements this month. You will start a new regimen, routine or a therapy which is going to help combat your health issues. This is a good thing and you should start it as soon as you can. You may be slightly worried about your health at the end of the month. But it will not be as bad as you think it will be. In fact, I see that your health is good and the situation is only going to improve.

May

This month, once again will be good for your health. All the shortcomings or difficulties that you have been facing so far, will be over. You will make a steady recovery and will settle into a more secure zone. You could be contemplating a change in terms of a short break or a holiday. Take it, for it will only rejuvenate you. I see you doing exceptionally well emotionally towards the end of the month. You will be feeling happy and content with life, and all your health wishes will come true.

June

A partnership or collaboration on health is in your cards this month. You may be getting into some kind of an arrangement to achieve a health target with either a healer or a therapist who can add value. You may be busy with family functions where happiness and love could pour in from all sides. This will keep you smiling and boost your mental well-being. You will need to remind yourself about your abilities and inner strength at the end of June when you may be battling a serious or chronic ailment. You are the magician who holds the power to your own healing. Just believe in your strength and wave the magical wand to see positive outcomes.

July

The month will kick off with some difficulty. You may be grappling a health condition which needs all your attention and strength. You will soon receive news that will tell you there is need for action. Get up and get going. You may need to change your treatment modality, start exercising and organize your diet and lifestyle to support your health. A better phase will start at the end of the month, when you will achieve your health targets. Your health will begin to show signs of improvement due to your efforts.

August

If the health situation has been difficult until now, it is likely to improve. You will be at your fittest best and you will be eager to work on your clearly defined health objectives. Mid-month, you will receive some rewards in terms of progress in your health, with your efforts coming to fruition. You may be getting ready to start a new regimen or routine once again. You know how to go about doing this and you will be raring to boost your efforts to reach this health goal.

September

You may be trapped in a situation in which someone is not being honest about your present health conditions. This person could be conning you in the name of treatment. Beware of a misdiagnosis. It would be a good idea to get to the bottom of the situation and clear up your doubts. As you move further into the month, the status quo will improve and you will make progress. In fact, you will begin to reap the rewards for your efforts. The end of the month, however, points to an emotionally challenging phase when you could have health issues because of repressed emotions or holding on to the past. Drop this emotional baggage and move on. The past is history; learn to forget it.

October

You will take control of your life and chalk out plans to meet your health goals this October. You may decide to embark on an initiative that is promising and exciting. While this journey is new and adventurous, there is a certain unknown element in it. You have never done something like this before and while this new treatment, therapy or routine sounds exciting, it has its own risks. A woman can help you strategize your way forward on this journey. She is a positive influence and you can rely on her.

November

There is a need to look at life more lovingly and compassionately. If you give love, you will get it in return. This approach will fill you with positive emotions and make your recovery simpler and quicker. I see your health improving as you move closer to your health goals. There is some news on its way to you, and in all probability it will be good news. You need to pay close attention to your body, because it may be communicating with you now. If you have aches and pains, there is a possibility that your body is trying to convey something important to you, such as letting go of negative emotions or embracing happiness.

December

If you are battling a chronic condition, you should remind yourself about the inner strength that lies within all of us. If you remain positive and fight, victory is guaranteed. However, in order to win, you will have to make a certain change in your life. This could be more like a compromise or a sacrifice such as watching your lifestyle, curbing all binging and working on your body through exercise, etc. Rewards of this compromise or adjustment will be ample, so you should seriously consider it. The year will end with you feeling demotivated and losing interest in your health routine. This attitude can be detrimental and it needs to be fixed immediately. Now is not the time to lose focus and attention.

Wealth Forecasts

January

January will present a competitive environment for your investments and assets. The market will be edgy and competitive, and in the given scenario your money is unlikely to grow. Avoid investing money or blocking your funds this month. Now may not be the time to invest in the market; instead it is time to simply watch how your existing investments perform. Someone kind will offer financial aid which may not be a windfall but will be a definite influx of money. When you get more, give that much more. This act of kindness is payback for your good karma. Enjoy the yields and use them prudently.

February

Your finances will take a beating and your stocks and investments will hit rock bottom. If you were expecting something or someone to turn up and alleviate this quagmire, think again – in all probability, this will not happen. This is not the time to gamble, invest or block your money. Stay prudent and watch your spends. A man who is sharp, articulate and intelligent could offer a solution or advise you in the manner needed. You can believe him. Changes will occur at the end of the month and the final outcome will be positive. You could consider being generous and share your wealth to attract more.

March

You will have to draw your attention to how you can use your creative abilities to develop an idea or an alternative source of income. Take up the offer of a compassionate and kind woman who is willing to help and give advice. The money will look good mid-March and you may decide to spend some on pampering yourself and indulging in luxurious pursuits. Do take out time to look into your past memories and contacts. There is an opportunity or an avenue there that lies unexplored.

April

Your finances are going to slow down this month. Payments will be stuck or overdue, your income will fall short and your expenses will be excessive. People and circumstances will be pulling you in all directions, but some alone time will bring forth clarity and offer a solution. The end of the month is an incredible time when money will seem to flow in from different directions. Whatever happened in the initial part of this month was temporary as I see your finances on an upswing.

May

Your finances will take a beating and your stocks and investments will hit rock bottom. If you were expecting something or someone to turn up and offer you a good opportunity, think again. In all probability, this will not happen. This is not the time to gamble, invest or block your money. Stay prudent and watch your spending. If you are in any kind of denial about your financial situation, it's time you took stock of it. Know that the situation is uptight and there is a difficulty which needs attention. A man who is sharp, articulate and intelligent could offer a solution or advise you in the manner needed. You can believe him. Changes will occur at the end of the month and the final outcome will be positive.

June

This month will mark your comeback. The financial environment will be competitive and your money is bound to grow. You will have to hang in there and wait until your stocks and investments rise to a certain point and then you can choose to sell or buy. This is a period when a wait-and-watch attitude will help. Financial aid will come in through the benevolence of someone who will be repaying you for some kind act you did in the past. There is also a reward coming in for your efforts at work. A bonus or a raise is in the offing.

July

July will start off very well with the possibility of better financial stability. You may be getting ready to change jobs, or probably someone intends to give you a gift of money. Finance is not a problem at all mid-month as I see you feeling abundant and content with your income and earnings. Instead of hoarding it in a bank, put it to good use. You could consider sharing your plenitude with the less fortunate. At the end of the month, your pecuniary decisions may be hampered by another individual. If you are awaiting something that rests in someone else's hands, then in all probability it will get delayed.

August

I know that you are expecting an escalation in your returns on investments, dividends or stocks, but somehow all this seems to be stuck in a rut causing ceaseless delays and incessant worry. Patience is the need of the hour. I see that you will initiate something new, an adventurous venture to invest your money or develop a new set-up that looks promising. This initiative is new and risky but it will be rewarding if you succeed. The end of the month will fetch happy times again as I see a good omen opening a portal to profitable prospects. You will receive a handsome sum for your work or from your business, and this will leave you feeling joyful.

September

A sudden revelation could plunge your finances to an all-time low. You will need a strong stomach to digest this but know that all will change as nothing is permanent in life. As you move further into the month, your fiscal situation will improve. Your money and investments will settle down and on the whole, you should experience a better phase than the start of September. Up ahead lies another small challenge when competition and pressure will pull you down. Depending on the market scenario, your investments and wealth may take a beating for a while.

October

You could receive an uncxpected grant or financial aid in recognition of all your hard work. I have been noticing a trend in your wealth readings where the card of generosity is followed by rewards. You will receive a piece of positive news, primarily from your career, in the form of bonus or incentive. However, if there is any big decision that you have to take, or if you are harbouring a suspicion of some kind, then it would be best you get to the bottom of it. Do not be in haste to decide; instead take your time and analyse well before you take the leap. Some alone time can be beneficial, even if it's just a long walk to clear your mind.

November

You may be tempted to splurge. This may also be the phase when you invest your money in wrong avenues. Watch your social circle for people who have a negative influence on you and misguide you. Your money is likely to grow this month. An uplifting positive outcome is around the corner. Your finances will respond well to the market scenario and will grow steadily. Your career will be looking good too, but look out for a risky phase that lies ahead. The last few days of the month will be an intuitive period where your instinct will guide you to take decisions. A woman may play an important role in your financial decisions. Look out for people who may not be completely honest about what they propose. If you feel something is amiss somewhere, investigate it.

December

You will be feeling complacent with your present financial situation. You have reasons enough to be happy, one of which is the new initiative that you may be about to embark upon. This initiative will be exciting and interesting and you will be thrilled about it. You will have enough money to spend on your loved ones, and you will be able to make arrangements for all the spending that you have earmarked for this month. Now if risky investments are bothering you, stay away from them. Don't throw away all the good that you have achieved so far. Do not make decisions unless you have total clarity. If you are expecting an influx of funds based on someone's decision, then you may be disappointed.

Career Forecasts

January

You may have bitten off more than you can chew and could be feeling defeated and overwhelmed. Although you are unable to withstand this pressure, in my opinion, since you have managed to come this far, you just have to hang in there just a little longer and you will break even. You may be getting ready to quit and moving on to a place where you are more appreciated. Keep in mind, the wheels of fortune will be turning in your favour mid-month, when an unexpected and very promising change will come.

February

You may be hopping from one place to another and surging ahead with achieving targets. I see you pragmatically shutting down something that may have failed. It will be a difficult but imperative decision to terminate the particular business unit, job or assignment. You could also be considering relocation to follow your dream, or in pursuit of a job which is aspirational. The last few days will see you juggling two jobs or two aspects of work or life which will take a lot of your energy. Multitasking will be the need of the hour. Respite will be on its way, but until it comes, continue multitasking.

March

The cards that predict the future in your career indicate that this is a time when holding on to hope can mean everything. Better prospects lie ahead and all you need to do now is to maintain the status quo. An older person such as a senior colleague, a male figure, could be a part of your work scene. He will guide you through the difficulties. Your career looks good where targets will be met but you will do better if you apply logic and some more discipline in the way you perform. If you have a tendency to fly by the seat of your pants, then it's time to reconsider your working style. A chance meeting with someone or something from the past could impact the present. Look to your past for hidden solutions to your career issues.

April

You will finally land your dream job. If you are already in an existing job, then it is going to get even better. You will be doing exceptionally well at work where targets will look easy, equations will be perfect and the timing can't get better than this. You will wonder how so much success has come so suddenly. But don't get carried away as you begin to become indispensable at your job. As you approach the end of the month, there is a possibility of ego clashes and miscommunication. You may not understand what's happening and your colleagues and peers may suddenly become distant. During such times, stay calm and try to find a solution with poise and composure.

May

If you are feeling bogged down, then this month may mark the end of your monotony. You are likely to change jobs and attract something more appropriate. There will come a stage when too much work will be on your plate and there will be too little time to do it. You may feel pressured but there is nothing much you can do about this except to roll up your sleeves and beaver on. The end of the month will see an overbearing man enter your work scene. He could be your senior or a boss who is both authoritative and efficient. You could learn a lot from him, but bear in mind that he may have a rough way to deal with people.

June

People in general will be browbeating you and you may have to prove your mettle. This will be a difficult time when focus and stability will be of prime importance. You may go through a phase when questions will be asked and your answers will have to be impeccable. Mid-month, something very important will come your way for which you have waited a very long time. If you have the tendency to mix romance with work, then it's best that you refrain from doing so. This could harm your career. The end of the month will mark a very good comeback for you when your work will be at its peak and you will be getting ready to initiate a new job, business or project.

July

A big change is coming your way this month. This may mean walking a tightrope for a while, and you may have to accept a pay cut, a role change to a lower cadre or even a job change which may not be something that you are happy about. There could be changes on a personal level where your ego may have to be curbed and you may be compelled to adopt a more conducive approach. I advise you to just go with the flow. This phase will bring its own set of doubts and ennui, and you may lose interest in what you are doing. Instead of questioning others, it's best to question yourself and find the solutions to your problems within. In the last few days of the month, you will be rewarded for your work. However, if you have been slacking, then be prepared to pull up your socks and prove your worth before you are questioned.

August

You may be trying too hard to do the right thing. With due introspection you may arrive at the answers. A big change is on the cards which will alter everything you have been doing so far. This may mean either a job change, role change or even a situation where you could leave or be asked to leave. If you have been working at a job that is completely wrong for you but provides you with a steady income, then this push to leave will be the best thing that could happen. There are better things in store for you. A woman will help you in planning your way forward in your career. She could be instrumental in helping you find a new position or to settle down in your existing role.

September

You could either be stuck in a job which is not right for you or you may be anxious about your job. If you feel you are stuck in a rut, then perhaps it is time you planned an exit. Good times lie ahead and I see a positive change once again sweeping you off your feet. This will bring in good prospects, success and advancement in your career. The end of the month will be a busy time with much work and action. In fact it will be more than you can handle. But all you can do is to get on with it and use all your resources to achieve the best possible outcome. If help is needed, don't hesitate to ask for it.

October

You have a strong, authoritative boss who may seem to be a difficult person to work with initially. He has rough edges, especially when it comes to his people skills, but that is something you can deal with. He will help you through your predicaments, and his influence will be positive. A crucial opportunity is in the wings. This could be a dream job or the opportunity which you have been waiting for. However, you will have to learn the ropes for this new task, role, job or professional course from scratch. This will be difficult because to learn something new you may have to first unlearn what you know. The pressure is going to be high, people will be watching you and, more importantly, you will have to prove yourself in this role.

November

A woman will hold an important position in your career this month. She cannot be trifled with and you will have to learn to handle her tactfully as she is key. You may be doing well in your career now and positive thoughts and energy will be taking you in the right direction. If you are in a job where you have spent a lot of time and are unhappy, then know that you are the only one who holds the power to change this situation. You may also arrive at the realization that something you are doing is failing to work for you despite all your efforts and hard work. If this is your state, then ending this association is sensible. You should call it quits and move on. Choosing to do so is going to be difficult but it is imperative.

December

You will be doing very well in your career except for a small issue where you could feel antipathy from someone in your work set-up. Don't fret over it, just let this person be and focus on getting your work to fruition. After all your success is what will speak for you in the long run. A woman will be crucial for your career now. She is kind and compassionate and will be willing to help you out. I see you adopt a more positive outlook towards your work, where you will begin to like and appreciate what you are doing. If you are looking for a job, then you will attract one soon. If you are in an existing work set-up, then circumstances are going to improve a great deal and there could be a possibility of a raise or an unexpected bonus or incentive.

CANCER

THE CHARIOT

Love Forecasts

January

Emotions of regret, guilt or failure are troubling you and this emotional baggage is impacting your relationship. You may have ended one relationship and are considering getting into another one, but the past is making it all difficult. Learn to let go and the situation will improve. If there are issues in a relationship, it's best to speak up and express your viewpoint firmly. Towards the end of the month, trust will become a crucial factor with either you or your partner being dishonest. The lies and deceit if any will soon be revealed.

If you are single and looking for love, then in January you will be immensely attracted to an older person who is disciplined, logical and likes structure. Don't rule out this person because of age.

February

You will witness stability, happiness and a new meaning to your relationship this month. Your relationship will rise to new levels of maturity and there will be a strong bond of love. Towards the end of the month, you may choose to stop something or initiate a new way of doing it, showing that your relationship is an egalitarian one, and you and your partner can exercise freedom of thought and expression.

The unattached Cancer should get ready to be swept off his/her feet in love. You are about to meet someone attractive and interesting.

March

If you are stuck in a stifling relationship which lacks freedom of expression or thought, it's time to break free and speak your mind. You are unhappy about something and are unable to do much about it. You may decide to end something and restart it in a manner that suits your needs. You will have to be more disciplined and practical in your approach towards your partner, and apply logic instead of emotions. Work on your relationship the way you work on other aspects of your life.

The single Cancer may have recently met someone exciting but this person may not be what he or she appears to be. You may be disappointed if you pin your hopes on this person.

April

You may decide to take your relationship to the next level and either move in together or announce a marriage or an engagement. This initiative is excellent and promises happy beginnings. But what follows will be disheartening. The issues in the relationship will fracture this arrangement beyond your capacity to repair. The last few days of the month will be marked by change. You will begin something new which is more worthy of you. April is going to be a challenging month and I pray you have a strong heart to deal with what lies ahead.

The unattached Cancer will be too busy with his/her career. With all work and no time to play, love may seem to be a distant possibility. I think you should make time to explore love before you miss the bus.

May

You may get restless and lose patience with your beloved, but hold on and trust your instincts as the situation is about to change. Patience is a virtue which will definitely come in handy this month. You will receive some good news mid-May when I see balance and equality in your relationship. Your past may play an important role in your present in the last week of this month. You or a former beloved may decide to get back together and ruin the harmony you have achieved in your love life. Keep this influence at bay and deal with the situation calmly.

If you are looking for love, then this month may not be such a good time to find it. In fact, it's best to stay low and focus on other aspects of your life which may be at a critical stage.

June

Both of you may be headstrong and approach this relationship from your individual standpoints. This may create some conflict and issues, but if you put your egos aside and discuss the problems, then I am sure you will find solutions. Your career may be taking too much of your time and energy causing issues in love life. A woman will play an important role in your life now. I see your greatest wish in love being manifested. This may mean marriage or a commitment which you always desired and which will leave you feeling happy and joyous.

The single Cancer is ready to be swept off his/her feet this month. You will meet Miss/Mr Right and initiate a journey of love.

July

If you have been facing issues in your love life, you will find that most of these worries will die down in July. I see you and your partner moving towards stability and peace. There is balance, love and equilibrium in your relationship. But you may find yourself getting bored by the end of the month, with love losing its lustre. You may need to look within and question your role in the relationship before pointing fingers at your partner. In fact, you have a great deal to be grateful for and you must consider counting your blessings.

The unattached Cancer may meet someone kind, generous and compassionate. This person will be an evolved individual with whom there is hope for a good start in love.

August

You are giving too much time to your career and while you may be busy strategizing and working things out at work, your love relationship may be taking a beating. It's best to give equal time to the various aspects of your life and set your priorities. If you are forced into something that you don't want, it's best to make yourself clear and communicate what you feel. The end of the month will be a magical time for love. I see that your instincts will guide you well and you may begin to appear very attractive to your partner.

The single Cancer may decide to take a short break to clear his/her head and feel rejuvenated. The good news is that you may meet someone exciting during this short break.

September

This will be a time of deep spirituality and you may be drawn to bringing a metaphysical perspective to your love life. This perspective is refreshing and will help stabilize your love life. You could also seek out a counsellor or a therapist who can help you and your beloved work on your relationship. The month will end with a good omen which will uplift your spirits and help you look at life in a positive way. This will give you reasons to be happier and content with what you have. Love will be going well for you and your relationship will be at its romantic best.

If you are looking for love, then you may rekindle a past romantic association this month. If this is not something you want, then reconsider your options and introspect on what you really want in love.

October

If there were issues in your love life before, there is peace and calm now. This should give you time to reflect on what you truly desire in a love relationship. If you and your partner are not happy in this relationship, then there will be bickering over petty issues. Both of you may decide to move on if the relationship is lopsided and doesn't hold much of a future. If you decide to end the relationship, then this decision shall bring forth a change that promises renewal and transformation, provided you move out of your comfort zone of a stable, albeit loveless, relationship.

The unattached Cancer may be juggling love with work and other important issues, and may be torn between them, which will delay the possibilities for love. To explore love, you need to be ready, and make time and space to let love flow in.

November

The situation may get heated and squabbles may occur, leaving you feeling sad and broken. This is not the time to take impulsive decisions about starting or ending a relationship. If you are having a clandestine love affair, then it may come to an end this month. Your relationship will take a turn for the better this November and it will see a happier and more balanced phase. There is good news coming your way which will seal the bond of love for you and usher in happiness and joy into your life.

If you are looking for love, your search will end this month. You are in for a life-changing event and the person who enters your life at this time will be the one for you.

December

You may learn of some not-so-good facts about your relationship this month, and realize that your partner doesn't care for you. This truth will leave you heartbroken and disappointed. A woman, either your mother or another woman, plays an important role in your love life. Limit her influence and that should keep the negativity at bay. In the last few days of the year, all will seem well for you. You may be busy in a celebration like a reunion or a party which will bring you and your beloved close once again.

The single Cancer may be in a hurry to start a love relationship. However, I wouldn't recommend a relationship now. Go with the flow and take things slow and easy.

Health Forecasts

January

If you are experiencing any symptoms, get to the bottom of the problem and fix it, even if it is something chronic and you feel like you've had this issue ever since you can remember and consider it merely a minor problem. You could be consumed by anxiety and could be feeling restricted and constrained. You must change this negative thinking and move ahead. All ailments, big and small, are manifestations of stress, pain and negative thoughts. You should be mindful of your thoughts and their impact on your health. The month, however, will end on a good note. If you are expecting test results, the news is going to be good.

February

There will be perfect harmony in your health this month. Moderation is the key to success, hence learn to balance the various aspects of your life. Eat right, sleep right, exercise in moderation and make time to meditate each day. While I see you managing the parity well, you may have some repressed emotions which are creating a problem for you. If you are holding on to old wounds and painful thoughts, you need to let them go and learn to forgive and forget.

March

This month once again points to managing your negative emotions and doing away with past baggage. You should let go and move on, and the best way to let go is to forgive. The good news is that I see you facing your repressed emotions and attempting to let them go. This will open the door to betterment and will immediately reflect positively on your health. The month will end with moderation as your new mantra. You will be moderating the different aspects of your life to strike a balance and stabilize your health.

April

A message about your health is on its way to you. The message may not be what you have been expecting. It is quite likely to leave you feeling disappointed and dejected. The month may end with you struggling to find a solution to your health problem. This may mean evaluating new options and going in search of what will produce the best results. But do remember to take a breather and relax when you need to. Perhaps if you focus and have faith that the solution will come, it will.

May

You are worried and preoccupied about your health issues. You want to understand why your condition is deteriorating. You will leave no stone unturned to find an answer to your problem. This may also mean that you will have to go into isolation for a while to ponder about your problem. Mid-month will see you juggling two or more aspects of your life like work and personal life. Try to balance these aspects to achieve better health. The month will end with your intuition guiding you to investigate your health issue in detail. At such a stage, if you are considering important treatments, perhaps you should take a second opinion and be 100 per cent sure about these interventions.

June

You may initiate a venture or a short-term collaboration with someone or something that will promise better health prospects this month. This alliance will guarantee results. It may be a health coaching class like yoga or the gym, or it may be a certain diet, ritual or marathon practice. You have too many options before you, with each one promising a health benefit. Choosing an option may sap your energy and peace of mind. Resolve the confusion soon by making a wise choice. The month will end with some imbalance and difficulties, with two difficult routines or rituals draining your energy. I believe it's best to choose one and let go of the other.

July

This month, you will reap the rewards for your efforts and I see you achieving your goals. If your aim was weight-loss, weight-gain, freedom from a chronic ailment or a desired fitness level, you will fulfil it this month. You will adopt a more optimistic approach towards life. This may mean looking at life more compassionately and lovingly. A woman will play an important role in your life towards the end of July. Her influence is positive and it will help improve your health. You could be getting ready to explore love and be more open to dealing with your loved ones in a positive manner. This will help you resolve repressed and difficult emotions.

August

This month is going to be gruelling with some health challenges. Be prepared to deal with them and put your best foot forward. Stay on your guard and do everything in your capacity to avoid the health issue before it manifests. The final outcome will eventually be good but do watch out for difficulties. A message is coming to you and it may not be something you hoped for. The month will end well with you approaching the problem more optimistically. Your health will begin to get better now and this will motivate you to stay positive. If you are expecting test results, the outcome you receive is likely to be good.

September

There is a need to be more disciplined and organized in your approach towards the well-being of your body, mind and soul. If you have been ignoring your diet, exercise or medication, it's time to get serious about it. You will end the month on a very positive note. I see you totally geared up and motivated to bring about the necessary changes to improve your routine. You will have a goal in your mind now, and you will be willing to channelize your energy to make it a reality.

October

You will be dealing with a lot of past baggage this month. Past is history and today is a gift, hence it's called the present. Let the past go and move on before this negative thinking begins to take a toll on your health. Mid-October, I see you very happy and content with your life. This volte-face in your approach is the result of one of your health wishes coming true. If you have desired something in particular such as a doctor, a treatment, or a goal, then you will get what you want. Nevertheless, do look out for people who may not be entirely honest with you about your present health condition. Stay away from people who are deceitful.

November

I see a healer coming into your life, who is more traditional in his/her approach. This healer may not be a doctor but someone who can make a difference to your health.

This month will generally be good for your health, and you will achieve your targets. You will be at your best and make progress on your existing ailments. There is a need to trust your healers or therapist. Your health is on an upswing and these people will contribute to your well-being.

December

You will turn to a woman who will come along and help you get in touch with your soft emotional side and heal your health issues. She is someone important and her presence will impact you positively. This is also the time to use forgiveness to resolve old emotional hang-ups you have with certain people, and relinquish negative experiences and emotions. I see you starting something new like a new health routine, yoga or tai chi, or maybe a certain diet that will help you improve your overall health and contribute to your well-being. This may mean that you work harder on this health routine and commit yourself entirely to it. The year will end on a positive note, especially if you have been trying to conceive. Pregnancy is on the cards for you.

Wealth Forecasts

January

The year will start with some good news with respect to your finances. Your spending will be perfectly matched with your income. This implies a perfect state of balance between the two. In fact, the year will bring some important news for you. Your financial tide is going to turn for the better. If you have had money issues and have been struggling so far, you will find that the good times are here again. You can expect money coming in this month. Use the influx prudently and put it to good use. If you are seeking ways to increase your income, then look into the past and you may realize a life-changing opportunity lies there.

February

You are in for some good news at the start of the month. This news may emerge from a new job opportunity. You may get a gift of money from an unexpected source. Mid-month, your efforts are going to pay off. You can expect a raise, an incentive or a bonus for all the hard work and labour you have put in. A certain defeat may come along towards this month-end, just when everything is going so well. Your investments in real estate may take a beating. You may feel defeated and lost when it comes to your returns as they may not match the results you expected.

March

You may be considering home renovations and may also decide to redo your office space to add a touch of luxury and the extra comfort that money can buy. Do this by all means, but do remember to borrow only as much as you can easily repay. The month will end with some financial tensions and pressures. It may not be the time to make business decisions unless you are absolutely sure about the outcome. Stay calm and avoid making big investments, or gambling. If your finances depend on someone else's decisions, then the news that comes forth may not be all that positive.

April

Your finances will be looking good at this juncture with an unexpected windfall. You should use this money well and put it to good use. Do remember to share your wealth with the less fortunate, which will make your wealth grow. Your investments will grow and earn good returns. But watch out for the end of the month when I see you embarking on a spending spree and upsetting the applecart.

May

A new beginning will lead to a source of income and revenue. This exciting initiative will help create more wealth and you are gung ho about it. The month of May will see you receive the fruits of your efforts. You may be in for a bonus, pay hike or an incentive. Your investments too will give you monetary gains around this time. But there is a need to apply restraint on unnecessary spending. If you tend to overspend and purchase unnecessary things, remind yourself that money is valuable and learn to value every penny you have earned through hard work.

June

You may be facing a tight situation with too little in hand and too many things you need to do with it. The thought of meeting all your expenses will overwhelm you. But worrying is not going to help now. Use your creativity and find some interesting ways to generate wealth. Positive news is on its way to you. This news may help you develop new sources of wealth, or involve an unexpected influx of money. At the end of the month, I see you receiving financial aid with a significant amount of money from someone for your generosity or kindness in the past.

July

Your thoughts are responsible for your current financial position. If you have negative emotions about your financial state, then it's time you realign your thoughts and think positively. A strong woman will play an important role in shaping your finances now. She is a positive influence; therefore you can heed her advice. Someone may not be entirely honest with you about money. This may bother you, and your intuition will guide you to investigate. There is a need to bring discipline and structure to the way you conduct your finances. If you don't have the habit of saving and are extravagant in your spending, then this may become a source of worry later.

August

Beware of theft or robbery, even if it's a small amount. There is also the possibility of someone lying to you and not being fully honest about the financial transactions that matter to you. You may feel cheated and deceived. This situation can be avoided if you decide to take control of the present moment and act cautiously. The next few days will mark the start of happy times as I see a financial wish coming true. This manifestation of a dream will be unexpected and will leave you feeling delighted. However, towards the end, confusion will ruin the joy as I see you torn between various options for investment. Take your time, think through the various choices and be absolutely certain of your ultimate decision.

September

You will receive an unexpected sum of money or you will extend this help to someone in need. A little further into the month and you may have to resort to a different course of action to make your payments on schedule. Money may be a little tight and you will have to be cautious about planning your expenses. If you have your own business, then it's time you aggressively start accumulating funds. If your finances depend on someone else, then this month will not be such a good time for new avenues to open up.

October

Your wealth will be on an upswing this month, so much so that you may decide to go on an international vacation or buy something aspirational. You will have enough to spend and enough to save. Your investments will earn you good returns. A good omen is around the corner. You could receive an influx of wealth from your business or work. This is not the time to take uncalculated risks. In fact, use caution and ensure you use the influx prudently.

November

You may get into a partnership or an association of some kind which promises quick bucks and good prospects. This association will be short-lived. You may get anxious and worried about your finances mid-month. There is a possibility that you are overthinking and speculating about this problem. Just relax. Most of your money-related insecurities only exist in your head. You are going to take up a big initiative at the end of the month. This has its own risks but also great returns. You have all the potential to make this happen and you only need to believe in this dream.

December

You may be approached for a loan but since there is little chance of repayment, you would be advised not to lend the money, even though this refusal will spoil your relationship with the borrower. Do not block your money if you are not sure about something. A woman will play an important role in shaping your finances now. She will guide you right and her advice will yield good returns. Someone is not being entirely honest with you about money. If this is the case, go along with your intuitions and scrutinize the situation until your suspicions are allayed. It's best to avoid gambles or taking major risks.

Career Forecasts

January

The year kicks off very well for your career. You may be on the brink of initiating overseas travel or an overseas assignment which promises better prospects and success. You could be considering a short break which is long overdue considering that you have been working relentlessly. If you are looking for a job change, then the change will be around the corner. Towards the end of the month, you may have to moderate the various aspects of your work to bring about complete transformation. You could be managing two bosses, two assignments, working two jobs, or could be torn between managing your personal and professional life. The key to success lies in your skills to moderate and transform.

February

Some news is on its way that which will help enhance your career prospects and generate more wealth. You will be eagerly awaiting this message, but the message that arrives may not be exactly what you were expecting. Some commitment or promise made to you may have been broken, and this will leave you feeling cheated and defeated. The situation will change and you will move on with time. You may be in a healthily competitive environment in which there are many formidable contenders vying for the position that you are eyeing. You stand a good chance to win the job assignment or the project you have set your heart on.

March

The start of the month will find you dithering between several options. The decision may revolve around a career choice, a choice between job offers or whether to quit or not. Introspect thoroughly before you take a call. You will be back in power and your career will once again be on an upswing. People will look to you for inspiration and guidance, and this will boost your confidence and give you a high. The month will end with you getting restless awaiting a result which is due, and the delay is making you feel insecure. Being patient is your only option as the decision isn't in your hands.

April

You will be busy juggling two important aspects of your career this month. You could be juggling two bosses, two projects, two kinds of jobs or two aspects of your life which is going to leave you feeling overwhelmed and tired. A male boss will be part of your work set-up this month. He thinks quite highly of your work, will support you and wants you to ask for guidance. This is also the time when your work will pick up both in volume and quality, and you will be doing very well. The month will end with a woman's influence. A woman in your team will collaborate with you in achieving good results.

May

You may be trapped in a dead-end job but hanging on for the security and comfort it provides. You know you can do better than what you are currently doing but are too complacent to move on. If you choose to continue in your current job, then know that this is your choice and be content. There is a man, could be your boss or someone senior, who cannot be trifled with. He may be tough and hard on you, but his intention is not to hurt you. If you are looking for a job, you may have to impress a man who is a decision-maker. The month will end with you making a fresh start somewhere. This may mean a new vocation or a job. The job will be challenging and demanding, and you will have to prove yourself.

June

A man will enter your work scene this month. He is someone authoritative, fair and just. He can be a huge help to you if you choose to trust him. There is a need to be disciplined, organized and logical in your work. A tendency to be slack or disorganized in your work will not go down well with the man who is watching you as your boss. He prefers a logical approach and an organized manner of work. You should structure your work to suit the needs of the organization. There could be a person who may be dishonest with you. Do not trust people easily and watch your back.

July

A woman at your workplace will offer you a helping hand and be your ally this month. The situation will be positive now and you will be performing well at work. However, in mid-July, there will be certain issues which will leave you feeling troubled. This is not the time to jump to conclusions or take hasty decisions. Avoid getting into a confrontation with your co-workers. Things may get heated very easily; and hence, it's best to avoid such a situation. The month will end well. If you are seeking a job, you will soon receive an offer. In the existing work scenario, the situation will improve and things will once again look up.

August

You may have to let go of your self-limiting beliefs and old-fashioned outlook. It's time to adapt to what the existing work scenario offers and accept a change which is nigh. If you are looking for a job, then it may very well come through now. What comes along may seem disruptive initially but it will set the course for a life-changing career. You should appreciate it and adapt to what lies ahead instead of being fearful and anxious. The month will end rather well, and your work will speak highly of your contribution and skills. You will have a great deal to be proud of, and this should boost your confidence and performance.

September

You may be trying too hard to do the right thing this month. If this is so, and you are unable to find a solution, take some time off and introspect on ways to deal with your existing situation. A short time alone can bring forth a lot of clarity. Your work will be going very well this month but if you feel that you are being underpaid, perhaps it's time to speak up and let others know your accomplishments. The month will end well with a work opportunity that you wished for coming through.

October

Your intuition may be guiding you towards an opportunity that will come along this October, but stay away from office gossip and all the negativity. If you get caught up in it, you may well be sucked in. There is a man who will step into your work scenario. He may be your boss or someone who could be a mentor. However, he is a man of logic and discipline and he will expect you to have the same qualities. Adopt these qualities to win over this man and earn a strong position in your workplace. Be wary of unscrupulous characters and people who play politics. There is a person or an incident that may break your trust and leave you feeling duped.

November

If you are expecting a raise, promotion or a job offer which has been stuck in the pipeline for quite some time, then know that there will be a further delay in its manifestation. During this time, you may be juggling two jobs, two bosses, or two projects which will cause you stress and tension. However, respite will come soon. The month will end on a positive note. A male boss or a mentor who is positive will help you out with your difficulties. He means well and can be trusted. You should work under his guidance and weave your way to glory. Your work will pick up and be on an upswing.

December

You will be getting ready for an adventure and will initiate a journey which implies a job, project, assignment or a new business that you haven't done before. In an existing work set-up, you may have reached a stage of being indispensable. You will be doing exceptionally well in your career but do not get carried away. Your work situation will bring forth a scenario which will be difficult, almost impossible to deal with. This could involve a project, an assignment or a business unit coming to a sudden end. You may have done everything in your capacity to save it, but now all that is left is for you to resign yourself to its culmination.

LEO

STRENGTH

Love Forecasts

January

Your love life will be moving into a more comfortable space this month. If you are in a committed relationship, I see stability, peace and calm. A change will greatly help this scenario. You could consider a short trip or a holiday, even for a day, with your beloved. This month is potent for love. You will receive a lot of attention from your partner. Marriage or an engagement could be announced, and you may consider taking the relationship to the next level.

If you are a single Leo, get ready to rekindle an affair from the past. Your strong chemistry may lead to a love affair.

February

If your career is keeping you busy, make time for love. The greater the communication between the two of you, the better it will be for your love life. You will be getting ready for a change that will be positive and help stabilize your relationship.

For the unattached Leo, there is a very high possibility of a love relationship starting this month. But I hope you don't jump into this relationship too quickly, and make a wrong choice.

March

If you are expecting a commitment from your partner, you may be disappointed. Not that your partner loves you any less, it just means that the time is not right for it. A strong and opinionated man will play an important role in your love scene this month. This could be someone you know or even your partner, and the best way to deal with him is to be patient and loving. You may feel trapped in a situation and unable to break free. Nevertheless, you have what it takes to change the status quo. Do so before it's too late.

The single Leo will have to moderate his/her life to make time for love, if it is a priority. You may have to balance the other aspects of your life in order to create space for love.

April

April will be about realizing your romantic fantasies. Your general well-being in all aspects of your life will reflect positively on your love life. This is the phase when your relationship will recover from the deficits it may have faced in the past. A change is about to come along and you may have to simply go with the flow. Adapting to this new change will not be easy.

If you are seeking love, then your search will end here. You will initiate a love relationship with someone you deeply desire.

May

You may realize that your partner, doesn't feel the same way as you do and this may leave you heart broken. If you feel bogged down and pressured by your partner to stay in a relationship which has no future, it is best that you follow your heart and clearly communicate your reservations.

If you are single, you will be lucky in love this month. The opposite sex, in general, will find you very attractive and will be willing to give a relationship a try. Make the most of this gracious period.

June

You may have a reunion with someone from the past. This may mean an old affair being revived or an ex-lover coming back into your life. But you need to know where to draw the line. In general, your love life will do well this month. A young person will be part of your love scene. There is some news around the corner which will bring forth happiness and bond you and your partner in love. Now is the time to yield the returns for all the effort that you have invested in your relationship so far.

If you are unattached and looking for love, you will need to examine your present lifestyle. You may be spending too much time at work, leaving you little or no time to explore love.

July

The two of you share a chemistry that will keep you bonded in love. A small change can establish more space for bonding. You could consider a change of scenery like a short holiday to some place nearby. The end of the month will be a period when you decide to take the relationship to a new level. This may mean an official engagement, marriage or some other important decision that will confirm your commitment to your lover.

The single Leo will be swept off his/her feet by an attractive person. This person is sharp, witty and charming.

August

August will usher in a good omen. You will be wholly in love and your partner will be willing to put the same amount of effort and affection into the relationship as you, to keep it going. But do look out for the work-related stress that may become a problem later in the month, as this pressure may begin to creep into your bedroom. Involve your beloved so that he/she feels close and part of your life.

If you are seeking love, then August will be perfect for you. Your chances of meeting someone with whom you can instantly connect are very bright. You may already know this person.

September

A woman will play an important role in your love scene this month. She is headstrong and highly opinionated. She could be your mother, sister or someone else who is close. But do limit her interference because her influence may not be for the good. The end of the month will be a challenging time when you may have to decide whether to continue in this relationship or strive for something better. If you choose to stay on, then you need to immediately communicate your intention to your partner and fix your mistakes before it's too late.

The unattached Leo will appear to be very attractive to the opposite sex. This is the right time to fall in love as you will attract many suitors.

October

If you and your partner are evaluating the scope of your relationship, then chances are that both of you may choose to go your separate ways. There could be an amicable separation that may come this October. The end of the month is a time of conflict and arguments. You may have to lie low and hear your partner out. There is so much negativity in this relationship that you may be feeling defeated and close to losing patience. However, now is not the time to pick fights. Instead stay calm and reflect on the current events and arrive at a firm decision which can permanently fix your problems in love.

The single Leo will be very busy with his/her demanding career. This will leave you with practically no time for love. This is not a good sign considering you want to fall in love.

November

Your relationship lacks the balance and harmony to keep it stable. You and your beloved are incompatible because you are on different wavelengths. There is no equality in this relationship and it lacks respect and freedom of expression. It's about time you worked towards correcting the imbalance and restoring the peace. Mid-month, you will be busy strategizing ways and means to fix the problems in this relationship. However, avoid desperate measures and work on these areas patiently. There may be some trouble towards the end of the month. You may be worried and anxious about something in your relationship. If you suspect foul play, speak up and discuss this concern with your partner.

The single Leo may meet someone interesting from work. This is going to be an exciting and interesting month for you.

December

Tarot points to a time when it is important to hold on to hope. If you are losing the last fragment of faith in your love life, then hold on, the situation will change. The card I see depicts positive outcomes. You need to be calm and withstand all the odds for the situation to improve. You may meet a counsellor or a therapist to help you with your love issues. As you move further into the month you may come upon a certain revelation about your relationship and lover which could disappoint you. This may break your heart. But change being the only constant, all will change in time.

The single Leo will find love in a person whom he/she has known before. This person has been part of your life, but you never really looked considered him/her as a potential lover.

Health Forecasts

January

I see you very happy and motivated at the start of the year when you may take a short vacation or a holiday that gives you the opportunity to connect with your inner self and embrace your health and goodness. If you are expecting test results, you are likely to get good news with the outcomes being positive. Towards the end of the month, you may start something new such as a fitness class, a diet regimen or a new routine which you will begin from scratch. This is going to be challenging and will require dedication and discipline.

February

The remedy for your health lies in your past. This is the month when your past contacts will emerge and help you realize that the cure to your repressed emotions may be in your past. You are about to have a new beginning. This may simply mean preparing yourself to adopt a positive outlook. This is excellent since all problems do begin in the head. Exercising is a very good option now but please do take care not to overdo anything. The end of the month will bring happy times when you will be emotionally stable and willing to accept what has come your way.

March

A woman will play an important role with regard to your health this month. She will help restore the balance in your life. This is also the time when, if you adopt a more compassionate and loving approach, most of your health issues will begin to recede. Give love to your body and your body will respond beautifully. If you doubt the test results you have recently received, don't hesitate to take a second opinion. It is possible that the person who diagnosed you may not have been completely honest. Be cautious with such people. You will embark on a new adventure towards the end of the month – perhaps a new health course associated with the gym or classes in yoga or meditation which you have never undertaken before.

April

If you have been holding on to negative emotions from your past, then it's time to let them go. Take each day as it comes. Old grudges and ego issues are all passé. Also around this time, avoid jumping to conclusions. Make sure you research well before you take a decision. Whether it is weight-loss, a certain fitness level or mental peace, you will achieve the outcomes you have been hoping for this month. If you are expecting some news regarding health, such as test results or treatment options, you may find that this search or outcome will be delayed further. You will have to stay calm and simply wait.

May

You will be doing exceptionally well at the beginning of the month; and in fact, I see you celebrating your success with your loved ones. You may receive some good news regarding your health this month. The end of the month is a time for patience if you are awaiting test results or the returns for your efforts in health; be informed that the results will come in due course, so there is no point in getting stressed out about it.

June

You could be getting ready to take a short break that will help you connect with your inner self and recharge. However, look out for a drastic turn of events that may occur in mid-June. This incident may be difficult to deal with initially, but once you have adapted to it, you may witness a transformation. I see you ending something to initiate a new journey in health. This may mean ending an ongoing health treatment or a relationship with a health practitioner to begin something that you believe will give you better health results. You could also be involved in some happy events with celebrations and parties that will energize you emotionally and enhance your sense of well-being.

July

You are going to start something new and exciting this July. The initiative that you take is about a certain health routine such as yoga or a therapy that will help you get back on your feet. What you have signed up for is not easy and will need a great deal of effort and commitment. A very kind, generous and compassionate man is going to shape your health for good. He could be a healer, of the traditional kind, someone who is soft-spoken and experienced. Do learn to look at life more positively and adopt an optimistic approach.

August

You will need to closely monitor your problems now. If the diagnosis is not right, or if you have doubts about your treatment, take action to fix these issues. I see you ending an arrangement that may have failed to work for you. This will leave you feeling disappointed and distressed. You will find answers to your problems in your daily routine, so ask yourself whether you are exercising right, sleeping right and eating well. The month will end with you on a rejuvenation break. This break may imply a short hospitalization for an ailment which is temporary in nature. This break could also imply a short time off simply to reflect on life and its outcomes.

September

If you are expecting test results, then you will receive some good news. This is wonderful considering what you went through in the previous month. But don't get too excited and eager to start a new initiative. Go slow and easy on your body and curb your impatience. Just focus on doing what you can and receive the fruits of your efforts in the fullness of time. Towards the end of the month, you will take on a rather adventurous new venture, attempting something you have never done before. This new development will add thrill and excitement to your life.

October

If you were deeply wishing for a certain health-related outcome, it will be manifested this month. If your life is currently out of balance then you need to correct this imbalance by making a quick decision that will help you retain peace of mind. Exercise right, eat right, sleep well and work smart. Try various combinations to strike the right mix. It's important to make time for yourself. If you are putting everyone's needs above your own, your body may suffer.

November

November is the month for discipline from the physical standpoint, and applying a logical and practical approach to other aspects of your life. If you have been lazy and ignoring the needs of your body, get on your feet and move about. Give your body the exercise it needs. However, don't overdo things either. The good news is that I see you achieving a goal or outcome which you so badly desire. This may be a treatment, a healer or a doctor, or an outcome that you have always wanted. This will leave you feeling happy and emotionally content. The month will end with you taking on too much work. If you are feeling overwhelmed, space out your work and make some time for your health.

December

A healer or a doctor is about to step into your health scene. He holds the key to your health's stability and success. But success will come only when you decide to take control of your life, bring about the necessary changes and work towards achieving betterment. You may have to take some immediate measures to ensure your treatment is on schedule. The year is about to end and this is the time when one tends to binge and overdo one thing or the other. In the last few days of the month, ensure you remain disciplined and do things right. If you have the tendency to become a slave to your vices and overindulge, then exercise self-control.

Wealth Forecasts

January

If you are someone who spends illogically without considering your income, then you should resolve to change this. Money will not be a problem as you move further into the month. In fact, you have more than enough to fulfil your needs and the needs of all those who are important to you. Towards the end of the month, look out for some disappointing news. If you were expecting your money to perform better, or your income to increase, then the outcome is not going to be what you expected. Avoid any major risks and gambling at this time. Neither your luck nor your state of mind will favour you at this time.

February

You may consider buying a house or shifting home on a rental basis. This house will be something that matches your expectations. Your finances in general will be on an upswing. There is good news coming your way in the form of an unexpected windfall which will open the door to greater wealth opportunities and money. Wealth from a lottery or gambling win are also a possibility this month. One of your greatest wish in wealth is about to come true as you end this month.

March

You may need to dig deep in your past to connect with something or someone who can guide you to greater wealth opportunities. It's also quite likely that you will come upon something or someone who will help you revive your old contacts and shape your future. If you are feeling insecure and fearful about your money position, then you might encounter situations which will harm your finances – after all you are what you think.

April

You are about to hit the jackpot. This windfall may emerge from an idea or an initiative which you may have undertaken to generate wealth. The cards that I see for this month depict some good times for you. In tarot, such a phase is called the time of the genie, implying a wish will be granted. Your money or wealth wish is about to come true. Don't splurge and fall prey to your indulgent side. Use this money wisely and well.

May

You may be late or fall short in your payments. You may have to think of alternative ways to make the payments that are due. If you are running a business, then now is the time to pursue your debtors and ensure the money comes in. A woman will play an important role in shaping your finances. You should consider her advice. There is a need to accept the reality of your present financial situation. You may be in denial about its gravity and may still be slacking off. Consider sharing your wealth, to bring wealth back to you.

June

Tensions and difficulties may prevail this month. It's best to look at your finances dispassionately and you will be able to see the positives and stay optimistic if you choose to. A little further into this month and you will learn an ugly truth – that your financial stability will get further delayed. You will have to avoid risky investments at this time. Stay low and stay smart. You need to be more logical in your approach and be patient. Wait it out calmly and know that the money you are expecting is coming, but may get further delayed.

July

You may have to keep your expenses in check and ensure they do not exceed your income. Your returns on investments will also be well balanced with what you have put away. You may have initiated a new job, an alternative career or a vocation which will open the portal to more wealth. Some positive news is winging its way to you, which will give you something to look forward to. You may be preparing for something big, which you know will lead to money and material happiness. Approach your finances by choosing to invest in safe and traditional avenues. Don't take large risks this month and invest within your limits.

August

There will be a gradual upward shift which is good. To manage your money better, get more disciplined, practical and logical in your approach and curb the extravagance. An older man may be part of your finance scene this month. He will come up with some concrete and important ideas to influence your money position positively. The best way to generate more wealth is to look for opportunities which could emerge from the past. You may come upon something or a person who can help you connect the dots and lead to something big.

September

You will move away from the bad patch you were in and settle into a more comfortable financial zone. A positive change may come along this month. You will initiate a new investment or a partnership with someone to generate wealth. This collaboration, although short-lived, probably not more than six months, promises good returns. However, you may face challenges at the end of the month. If your financial outcomes depend on someone else's decision, your prospects may get further delayed. Avoid any risky decisions now and do not invest with the intent to make a quick buck.

October

You may receive an unexpected sum of money this October. This may come from a friend or a family member, or an inheritance. It could also just be a gift to you. This news will put you in a happy frame of mind and impact your financial situation positively. You may be preparing to receive the rewards for all your efforts at your workplace. If you are an entrepreneur and had approached a bank or any other financial institution for a loan, then it is likely to be approved this month.

November

A woman will play a crucial role in shaping your finances this month. If you can adopt an open mind, then you can learn from her. You will need to manage your business better or avoid considering more than one financial avenue for investment purposes. Make up your mind and take a decision which is backed by research and this will guarantee safe returns. Avoid investments for which you lack conviction and haven't done thorough research. The month will end with your financial state attaining balance. There will be parity between your income and expenses.

December

After a long period of uncertainty and upheaval, your finances are about to change for the good. You have worked very hard through the year and now is the time to reap all the rewards. There is perfect balance and harmony in your wealth situation and enough money to take care of all your expenses. You will also be able to save some. During the last few days of the year, you may decide to take on a new venture such as a job, a vocation or an investment avenue, for which you may have to work very hard initially. Until you have settled in and won everyone's confidence, there will be no reduction in pressure.

Career Forecasts

January

Your work may undergo some stress in the initial part of this month, when the work pressure will be too high and, more importantly, you will find yourself being closely monitored. The situation may get a little heated but stay calm, focus on your work and stick to your deliverables. By mid-month the difficulties would have settled and you will begin to move into a more comfortable position at work. A woman may come along and help you out. If you are beginning to feel disheartened with the work situation, then know that positive outcomes are in the offing.

February

A man who is authoritative and articulate will influence your work this month. He could be your senior, and is someone who can't be trifled with. He lacks finesse when it comes to dealing with people so handle him well as he is the key person in your career now. There is stiff competition for the job or role that you are seeking, with plenty of good candidates striving for it. But competition is fair and you are likely to do well. I see you taking up a new assignment or a job at the end of the month. This may entail learning new skills and understanding the requirements of the new job.

March

You will be working through your professional issues this month and I see you doing well and establishing a good position. A woman may once again play an important role in your life. It could be the same person who appeared in February. She will offer some critical solutions which will ease a lot of your work stress. Some news is on its way, which will help you feel better and realign your thoughts to positive outcomes. A change is on the cards – this may be a short break or a change in your job scenario – and it will lead to positive developments.

April

The path to better opportunities lies in your past. You may come upon a memory, a person or something that will make you nostalgic and help you connect the dots. Exploiting your creativity is another very good way to improve your potential at work. You will achieve your goals this month. Your targets and deliverables will be on schedule and you will feel a sense of accomplishment from doing everything right. However, if you feel underpaid or feel that you deserve a raise for your performance, this is the best time to speak up and make yourself heard. The end of the month may be a slightly difficult phase for you, when I see you feeling very restless and insecure about your position.

May

Your dream will come true this month and I see your greatest career ambitions realized. This will be an unexpected achievement and will leave you feeling triumphant. With this achievement will come a celebration. You will be back in the game and people at work will be looking to you for guidance and inspiration. You have raised the bar and this accomplishment truly deserves to be lauded.

June

Rewards will be raining down on you this June. You will receive a pay hike, an incentive or a bonus for your achievements and contributions. However, you will face some difficulties at work later in the month and will need to stay calm and continue to moderate opposing elements that impact your work to bring about synergy. These opposites may mean people in general with whom you are caught up in a fix at work. Trying out various permutations and combinations, but moderating opposing elements (people) will help. Towards the end of the month, your work will pick up again and you will be back on the achievers' list. But do not slack off now because you need to maintain the top position that you have achieved.

July

You may be stuck in a situation in which only your intuition can show you the way. Pay attention to it and let it guide you. This is not the time to get involved in office politics and gossip. You may develop absolute clarity about your job, which means a realization that you should move on or appreciate where you are for what it gives you. You will be in a dilemma whether to stay in it or leave it. The good news is, towards the end of the month, you will have clarity on what you want and will be ready for a big change. For all you know, you may decide to finally quit this place.

August

I see that your job scene is going to look positive with you either getting a new job or achieving a breakthrough in an existing job. Both money and success will come to you. If you sense a problem at work, then I suggest you get to the bottom of it and resolve it. It is good to do thorough research and put your doubts to rest before you commit to a project, person or job. The good news is that a male boss or a mentor will be supportive of you this month and you can trust him. He will guide you through your issues and help you out to the best of his ability. If you are wondering how people perceive you and your work, then my answer is that you are perceived as a good resource who can make a difference.

September

A very powerful and kind person will offer you a helping hand in your career and enable you to be more visible and useful in your workplace. If you are seeking a bank loan for your business, then the institution you approach will grant it to you. While your work will be looking very good and you will be at the top of the hierarchy at your workplace, you may have to work twice as hard to maintain this position and continue to prove your worth. The month will end with money and rewards raining down on you.

October

You may face a crucial decision for which your mind and heart will be conflicted. It's imperative that you make a fair choice after due diligence and analysis. This choice could be related to a new position, job or a role which has emerged in the most unexpected manner. As you move into the month, I see you making the right choice and landing a job or position which is perfect for you. Mid-month, you may find yourself in the doldrums where there is no work at all. This will make you feel powerless and disheartened. In my opinion, this situation will pass in time; you need to stay positive and hold on to hope.

November

If you find yourself stuck in a job that you have been doing for years, the cards that I see depict hope and good things coming your way. Your time will soon come. You need to be hopeful and look at the bright side of your career, or the job that you are in. The bad patch will be over mid-month, and the situation will only improve from here on. But watch out for small disappointments and subterfuges. You may feel cheated due to a broken promise or a commitment gone wrong. Someone may hurt your ego and this will make you feel defeated.

December

You may have to follow your instincts to deal with the situations and problems that lie ahead. Do what you feel is right, and do not ignore your intuition. Avoid office politics. You may be countering feelings of being stuck in a job, which isn't great, and which makes you feel unappreciated. You may be in it for the salary or the prospects it offers. However, look beyond it; there are good opportunities available outside if you make up your mind to move on. The month will end on a positive note and you will be in a state of balance. If you are looking for a job, then it's coming your way, especially an overseas opportunity. In the case of an existing work scenario, you will be in control of your thoughts, emotions and your work.

VIRGO

THE HERMIT

Love Forecasts

January

If you are in a committed relationship, you will experience boredom and a loss of lustre in your love life this month. The spark is missing and the chemistry is practically non-existent. Not that this is going to be permanent, but if change is what you are seeking, then you must openly convey your reservations to your partner. The situation may get more difficult further into the month, and you will have to stand your ground. Speaking your mind gently and graciously will help your relationship.

The single Virgo is very goal-oriented and will be ready to take on the challenge of finding a lover. This is the goal you have set out to achieve and I see you raring to work towards it.

February

You are at a point in love when your relationship could be coming to an end. This is upsetting and if you are absolutely certain that you don't want this to happen, you will need to work on your love life before it's too late. The next few days could bring some disheartening news which will leave you feeling shattered. If you are awaiting an answer from your partner about keeping the relationship going, then you may have to wait a while longer. Remember that you can't force your choices and decisions on others.

If you are single and finding it difficult to find love, then ask yourself if you are still stuck in the past with memories of a former lover or baggage holding you back from going all out to find true love.

March

There is a possibility that a former lover may come back into your life and your old romance may be rekindled. You need to assess where this relationship will lead you. Evaluate the consequences of your decision. Your existing relationship needs all your attention, and any deviation from the present may be harmful. The good news is that your relationship will rise to new levels of stability and maturity in the middle of the month.

If you are unattached, then chances are you will meet an interesting person this month. You will need a whole new strategy to lure this person.

April

April will be characterized by differences in love life. You may be feeling lost and defeated because of your partner's aggressive attitude. Although you may be prompted to fight back and prove your point, it would be best advised to stay calm. Your relationship will soon stabilize and begin to improve in terms of compatibility and understanding. However, if you and your partner are contemplating an amicable separation after considering all your options, then you may find that the time is right for this at the end of this month.

If you are single, someone will appear in your life through your past contacts – someone you already know but never perceived as a potential lover.

May

To make a relationship last, you may have to make certain changes or sacrifices. These sacrifices and changes may be difficult to adapt to initially, but in the long run they will benefit your love life. I see marriage or an official announcement indicating a commitment in your cards. You will be happy about this decision which I believe is a good start. You will need to balance your career with your love life. You may have to spend a lot of time at work which will adversely impact your love life. Make time for love and communicate with your partner.

The single Virgo will meet a suitor this month. Love is in the air and will enter your life soon.

June

If you have been awaiting an important achievement in your love life, then it will occur this month. This could be a marriage, a commitment or the love of a desired partner. You will be overjoyed to realize your dream and this will set the course for a new beginning. A change is on the horizon, something which will bring happiness into your life. If you have faced issues so far, the situation will change.

The unattached Virgo is in for some positive developments. You are likely to meet someone new and exciting this June.

July

Your relationship will get better, or you may already be witnessing greater stability with everything that you desire for your love life. Your love life will rise to new levels of happiness and maturity by the month end when you may be on the brink of taking a leap of faith. You may consider marriage or some other arrangement to indicate your complete commitment to the relationship. This decision carries some risk but you will be ready for the adventure and the challenges that come along with love.

If you are seeking love, then someone will enter your life soon. Be ready to be swept off your feet. Before you even realize it, you will be head over heels in love.

August

Don't let the ghosts from your past haunt your present. You should count your blessings and cherish the strong bond you share with your partner. I see happiness, joy and completion in your love life as you reach mid-August. The month will end with your greatest wish in love being granted.

The single Virgo will find himself/herself in an interesting phase, with suitors falling at your feet. You should make the most of this phase, but choose wisely and act with vigilance.

September

There is stability, parity and happiness. In fact, you have all that one could wish for. The one you care deeply about reciprocates your sentiments and will be willing to go the extra mile to make you feel special and desired. However, you may have to watch the time you or your partner spend away from home. This phase needs focus and attention because your careers may make it difficult for both of you to spend time together. Your work–life balance needs fine-tuning before it disrupts the equilibrium you both have strived to attain in your love life so far.

The single hermit will begin a new journey in love. A love affair, marriage or an official engagement is on the cards and will be announced soon. Although you are sceptical, you are willing to take this leap. Trust your instincts and go for it.

October

A woman will play a crucial role in your love life this month. She could either be your partner, mother, sister or a friend. You will need to adopt a positive approach towards your love life, especially to what lies ahead. There is a card of deception or treachery in your reading this month. This means that either you or your partner may be involved in foul play, and this is likely to surface this October. Towards the end of the month, you and your partner may decide to part ways for these and other reasons. Going your separate ways is likely to be the only option left for you in this situation.

If you are seeking love, then you won't have to look far as a message of love is about to reach you. You will need to pay attention to it and connect the dots to arrive at what you desire in love.

November

You may consider marriage or some other formal commitment to take your love to the next level. However, life doesn't always go as smoothly as one would like. You may be battling a difficult situation in another part of your life which will begin to take a toll on your relationship. Your work, which you may have just started, will take a toll on your time and energy, leaving very little room for love. But you need to bear in mind that constant effort and time is needed to keep any relationship afloat. Don't let these new developments impact what you have achieved in your love life.

I see an adventurous and energetic suitor in the single Virgo's cards. You are in for some happy times with love keeping you busy this November.

December

I see you achieving perfect balance and harmony in your love life this December. You and your lover will share a deep bond of love, with equality and freedom of expression playing an integral role in it. If you are a female Virgo, your partner will play an important role in shaping this relationship. He or you will be at the forefront, strategizing and making plans for the future. This is a good sign which denotes stability and success. I see the card of the genie which denotes happiness, love and joy that comes when a wish is granted and which will happen this month.

The single Virgo will end the year on a good note and will manifest true love, which will set the course for a new and happy beginning.

Health Forecasts

January

You may be very keen and serious about giving up old habits which have been detrimental to your health. Resolving to achieve better outcomes is a good way to start the year. If you are expecting test results, then the news is likely to be good. However, your health practitioner may not have diagnosed your existing health issue correctly, and may not be giving you the right treatment. You may have to get a second opinion or find a doctor or a healer who can help you with your ailment. You could consider taking a short vacation to feel rejuvenated and refreshed. You should begin to feel better towards the end of the month and your health will improve.

February

You may be overdoing something or performing below par in certain areas, which could be adversely impacting your health. If you are doing two things at a time, and this is creating an imbalance in your life, then it's best to focus on one of the two activities. There is a need for balance in your life right now. Emotionally, you have to watch where you are headed. If you are inclined towards substance abuse, you are strongly advised to stay away from this temptation. If you suspect an incorrect diagnosis or treatment, then follow your intuition and consider a second opinion. Ask for help if you need it. It is advisable to visit a counsellor who can help you reform and stabilize. Focus on maintaining a positive state of mind.

March

A traditional healer or counsellor who is conservative in approach will use his spiritual knowledge to alleviate your health problems. Your health may not be all that good this mid-month. You may be at a stage when the situation may get out of hand. This phase may seem to be the beginning of the end, but you need to believe in yourself and in your fighting spirit. Hang in there; miracles can happen. The month will end with some good news. I see you receiving help which will either come in the form of financial aid to facilitate your treatment, or a person who is a doctor or a therapist who will come forward and treat you in the manner needed.

April

You may be awaiting test results or some information about an existing ailment and its diagnosis. However, the delay in the arrival of the detailed report or diagnosis will leave you feeling restless and impatient. If you have been concerned about your health in general, then there is going to be some news which will help you understand the root cause of your health issues. The news is likely to be in your favour. The month will end with you going through a stressful period as you juggle the professional and personal aspects of your life.

May

There is a chance of a minor injury occurring this month. Be extra careful if you are involved in a physical activity, and avoid overdoing any exercise or routine now. If you are injured, then go extremely slow in re-building your strength. A change will occur this May. You may have to alter your lifestyle for the betterment of your health. The month will end with a kind and loving woman playing an important role in shaping your health. You should turn to her for affection and love which will heal you on a mental and spiritual plane.

June

If you are searching for solutions for your ill health or your present health condition, then don't get invasive treatment but seek answers in your daily life. See what you can do in your daily life to bring about a positive change in your health. You could alter your lifestyle and eat right, sleep well, exercise daily and stay positive. Mid-month, you will start a new routine, regimen, class or therapy which will initially seem challenging but will also be exciting and enjoyable. As you move closer to the end of the month, you are reminded to re-examine your emotional wounds which may not have healed over time. Processing these repressed emotions and letting them go will bring some respite and heal you on a spiritual plane.

July

You will see significant improvement in your health if you have been suffering from an ailment. You have done well so far and you should continue to put in the effort to stay fit and healthy. You will get good news if you are expecting test results, and this will further lift your spirits. However, you may face some sort of dilemma towards the end of the month. Your intuition will prompt you to reconsider your existing health practitioner's diagnosis and treatment. This will cause you some amount of stress. If you have a history of mental health issues, then do not ignore your intuition now. Also stay away from any kind of substance abuse which could lead to serious problems later on.

August

This August, you will end an association or a relationship with someone or something that you thought could better your health. You could also be troubled emotionally and should try to stay calm and handle the situation with a relaxed state of mind. Your health will change course in the coming days and you will make gradual progress. You will receive positive news regarding your health this month. The end of the month is a very happy time when you will receive the rewards for your hard work. There will be a big improvement in your health, and this outcome will not be a miracle but the fruit of your labour.

September

If you have doubts about your doctor or healer's diagnosis or treatment, then get to the bottom of the problem by taking a second opinion. If trust is an issue, then work to find a solution. Your health may face some problems due to unnecessary stress and tension this month. Work on these emotional issues by staying positive and adopting a logical and practical approach. You will have to use reason over emotions. Order and discipline can go a long way in tackling this issue. Plan your routine and be disciplined in following it.

October

Try to strike a balance between your personal and professional life, and give equal focus to exercise and diet, healthcare and meditation to heal your ailment. You will see positive results if you manage to strike the right balance.

You are all set and excited about initiating a new beginning. This may be a new treatment, health routine, or some kind of fitness class or course. It's time to put all your tensions aside and indulge in some play time. Don't take life too seriously and adopt a lighter perspective on life.

November

You will decide to take a break that will help you rejuvenate and recuperate. This break may be at a retreat or some time spent alone. This break could also be in the form of a short hospitalization. You will soon start an exciting journey and may choose to do something adventurous which you have never done before. This may be a new therapy, training or health course which promises excellent results. The month will end with you embracing an attitude of moderation in your life. You will moderate your eating habits, your sleep time, working hours and exercise regimen.

December

Something may not feel right and you may suspect the treatment that you are undergoing. Well, if your intuition is telling you to confirm your diagnosis, then you should do so. You may receive some disappointing news in the middle of December. This negative news will leave you feeling shaken and disheartened. You will begin to make a recovery as you draw closer to the end of the year and move towards stability and peace in health. The year end is the best time to take a break which will refresh you and set the ground for what lies ahead.

Wealth Forecasts

January

There is a need to balance your expenses with your income. If you are planning a major expenditure, then put this on hold for now. I recommend that you don't invest big or block your money this month. If you are ambivalent about two aspects of your finances, then choose to go with one of them and leave the other one. Managing two at a time is nearly impossible and can take a toll on your finances. Despite these odds, I see you doing fairly well by the time you reach the end of the month. You will enjoy a stable financial state and could be considering shifting home or purchasing a home.

February

A woman will play an important role in shaping your finances this month. You should consider her opinion and follow her advice. You may receive financial aid from a person who will repay your kindness with money, or a bank loan you had applied for may come through this month. It is also possible that you will lend money to someone who is in need, or do a charitable act. There will be some delay in the returns that you have been expecting. If you are awaiting some news that is related to your finances or investments, then it is likely to be delayed further.

March

Some news may come along that will rattle you a bit. Don't hesitate to ask for help if needed. Market fluctuations may impact your finances so staying put would be wise. Don't make any big or expensive investments as this is the time to allow your money to stabilize. Stay guarded and be certain about your financial decisions. There is some positive news coming your way. There is a possibility of better prospects hidden in this opportunity, and I see you excited and agog.

April

You can expect a raise, incentive or a sudden influx of wealth from ancestral property this month. This will stabilize your financial position and give you more than enough to fulfil your needs and to save. Invest wisely in the future and watch your money grow. You could be evaluating the idea of home renovations and repairs. Investing in comfort and luxury is a good thought, provided you exercise caution, moderation and don't overspend. Spending money mindlessly will put you in a difficult spot.

May

You will experience a perfect balance between your income and your expenditure. You will be cautious about the way you are using your money, which is a good habit that you have developed over time. Your investments will be growing and performing well. You should plan for your future since your present is looking so good. But while you will be busy making money, do remember to share some of it with the less fortunate.

June

This month will start well and I see you receiving rewards for all your toil. Mid-June, exercise caution in your investments and spending. If you are tempted to take a big leap, do thorough research and back it up with conviction. Your intuition may sense something fishy about someone or something. If you doubt someone's intentions and feel that he/she is not being entirely clear about some investment, then avoid bankrolling the venture with this person altogether. You will receive some disappointing news towards the end of the month. You may realize that an opening or an opportunity that you were banking on is not working out.

July

You may be evaluating the options of purchasing an automobile or even an expensive holiday ticket for you or your family. You will be considering some renovations in your home or office space. Moving from comfort to luxury is a good thought but ensure that you will be able to repay your mortgage and other expenses. You may reach an all-time low at the end of this month, and you could begin to doubt your potential to make and save money. But know this – the situation is temporary and is bound to change with time.

August

You will begin to improve financially and make gradual and steady progress on the path to full recovery. Right now, your focus should be on saving as much as you can. The news will be good even in the middle of the month. Your finances will be on an upswing and I see the wheel of fortune turning in your favour. This implies a sudden turn of events and the onset of positive outcomes. The situation will unexpectedly work in your favour and resolve your financial difficulty.

September

You will receive some news which will shatter your dreams related to your financial plans. What matters is how you handle yourself through it. A very authoritative and powerful man could be part of your finances this month. This is the time to consider starting your own business. You could also discover a hidden talent which may surface in you now. Use these findings to help you establish something worthwhile. The month end will not be such a good time to take risky business decisions or to take a big financial leap. You will have to follow your instincts and have complete conviction in your decisions.

October

You will receive positive outcomes and money will begin to come in. An opportunity or an avenue is going to open up this month which will let you generate money and create wealth. But to do this, you need to believe in your capabilities and have faith in your potential. The month will end on a good note with money on its way to you. Use it prudently, not for gambling or other wasteful spending which will create a financial issue for you once again. It is best to be careful and put the money you have earned to good use.

November

If you believe that your luck in money will always be bad, then this is what it will be. Hence, it's important to tweak your mindset about money to a positive one. Middle of the month will be a very positive period for you, as I see the blockage which you may have been facing clear up. It would be best to exercise caution and moderation in spends. Using this money on risky investment plans or gambling is the last thing that should be on your mind. It is also possible that you will be approached for a loan; in my opinion, the loan is unlikely to be repaid. Hence, it is best that you don't lend any money, at least not in November.

December

If you don't trust a person or an opportunity that has come along, then simply stay away from it. It is best to use your money on opportunities that you trust. You may be generally anxious and worried about what will happen next, and this may be causing you sleepless nights. In the last two weeks of the month, you will witness a better phase. You will have enough money to fulfil your wishes and those of your loved ones. Your investments will perform exceptionally well and will yield the best returns. I see you ending the year happily with your loved ones, at least in terms of your finances.

Career Forecasts

January

You will receive rewards and recognition for all your efforts at the start of this year, which will mark a wonderful new beginning for you. Later in the month, you may receive a job offer or change your role or project. This development looks promising and you are excited about what lies ahead. The month will end with you trying to maintain a balance in your life. The balance at work will entirely depend on how you manage people at various levels. You will also have to manage your work and other aspects of your life.

February

You will be starting a new project or a job which will give you all the thrill and excitement that you want. An authoritative man will be part of your work scene this month. He may be a senior or a mentor of some kind. At work in general, you will start off by doing well, but do watch out for what will come towards the end of the month. You could clash with your co-workers because of a difference of opinion on ideas and innovations. This may create a difficult phase for you. You should try and handle the situation as calmly as possible and realize that everyone can't think like you. If you are seeking a job, then adopt an attitude of humility when you go for interviews.

March

You will earn recognition and rewards for your contributions and generally fly high at your workplace. You would have had to put in a lot of hard work to reach the top, and now you will have to put in considerable effort and focus to stay there. You and your seniors or colleagues have opposing views and this could lead to a conflict. There is also a very high possibility that you may be discredited and disregarded for all the work you have put in, and someone else may take the credit due to you. The month will end well and I see you achieving all the goals and targets assigned to you. This success will make you confident and help you win accolades again.

April

A man is going to play an important role in your career this April. He may be your senior or a boss who can influence your work. He is highly opinionated and clear in his thoughts, and is someone you can't trifle with. If you are looking for a job, then know that there is stiff competition with several formidable opponents vying for this position you are seeking. The month will end with your energy levels being at an all-time high. You will be highly driven to achieve what you wish to in your career.

May

You are going to get lucky with a raise or a better position this month. If you are looking for a job, then it may come through now. Mid-month, you may face a minor dilemma and be left with no choice but to juggle the various aspects of your career. This may mean multitasking and juggling two jobs – one, your regular job and the other, a hobby – or two projects, two bosses, or two aspects of life such as work and your personal life. The month will end with some good news. You will see an end to this multitasking and make greater headway in your career.

June

If you have been thinking or dreaming about a certain job, a pay raise or a role, then your wish is about to come true this June. You will accomplish something very important in your career, which has seemed nigh impossible so far. Stay logical, be practical and disciplined towards your work. A man senior in authority or age will help you shape your career this month. The month will end with some good news if you are looking for a job. Relinquish your conservative beliefs and your obsolete approach and you will fit in better with your avant-garde work environment.

July

It's possible that you have been placing greater emphasis on either your personal life or your professional life, which is why you may be off balance. It's best to divide your time and energy equally between the various aspects of your life. Something may not be right at your workplace mid-month. I see you calling it quits after trying every possible method of keeping afloat a certain project, work relationship or job. The month will conclude with your search for a better opportunity. You may have to be patient as the news that you are expecting with regard to a job change, raise or a bonus is likely to get further delayed. But know it is only a matter of time and it will eventually come through.

August

You will be getting ready to accept a new job offer this month. A mentor or a teacher is likely to come along this month. This person is helpful, kind and mostly traditional in approach but his/her guidance will bring in a much-needed perspective to your career. Alternatively, you may have to play the role of a mentor to someone at this time, which means that you have graduated to a level which gives you the confidence to counsel another person. A woman with a calm demeanour and gentle approach will facilitate your metamorphosis into a guide. August is also the month when you must focus on your emotional and creative side. Use your creative intelligence to harness a great idea and turn it into reality.

September

If you have been working hard, then know that the fruits of your labour are on the way. However, if you have been indolent and complacent, then it's time to get serious about your work. A man will play an important role in your life now. This person could be your direct senior or a person who is very high up in your organization's echelons. If you have been wondering what people think about your work, then know that you are considered a good resource. In the middle of September, you will need to learn to let go. Do not hold on to personal grudges or remarks that people make about you or your work.

October

Put your best foot forward and work mindfully to be more productive and avoid making mistakes. Hold your ground as the situation is going to get a bit rocky. However, the good news is that beyond this phase lies success. I see you getting the raise, bonus, increment or role change that you desire but didn't expect to get this month. At the end of the month, you may have to do some amount of juggling between two jobs, two departments or two bosses. You are good at multitasking and your ability will be put to the test now.

November

You will be holding on to the emotions of the past this month. Now is the time to focus on your present. Do not waste time over spilt milk; instead look at the plethora of opportunities that lie ahead. You may be about to initiate an association with another person or an entity. This initiative will be short-lived but it promises success and prosperity. You could be getting ready to leave your existing job for something better that has come along.

December

You may undertake travel which is work related, and this will leave you feeling excited and elated. This travel may be mostly domestic but it will give you the opportunity to network and expand your contacts. Some good news may be around the corner if you are seeking a job. In an existing work scenario, you will be doing rather well. But don't take this success for granted. Reaching the top is difficult but maintaining that position is even more challenging. Your negative thoughts about your work environment may be making you your own worst enemy. Nevertheless, realize that the set-up can't change and your co-workers will not adapt to your viewpoint. So you may have to work hard to adapt to the dynamic situation at your workplace. Around the end of December, you may face a conflict which will take an ugly turn, leaving you feeling defeated and discredited. However, all this will change in 2019 if you choose to stay calm.

LIBRA

JUSTICE

Love Forecasts

January

The past may intrude into your ongoing relationship this month. A former lover may emerge out of the blue which could lead to something unknown and unexpected. I see you excited, eager and willing to do what is necessary to take your relationship to the next level. However, there is a chance that one of the two partners in the relationship may begin to feel trapped and saturated. To salvage your love life, it's best you speak up and clarify your position, and understand your partner's needs.

The unattached Libra will find love in an old acquaintance. This will lead to a fresh start.

February

Your relationship will be going swimmingly this month, and both you and your partner will be willing to give love and receive it in return. There is a possibility that one of you will offer financial help to the other. There will be a small problem though, amidst all this love and equality. A woman could influence your relationship negatively. This woman may be your mother, sister or a close friend who will influence you or your partner with negative ideas about love. You must take control of the situation and know where to limit her interference.

The single Libra will get out more and meet new people. This is a good way to start your initiative in love as the more you socialize, the more you widen your horizon to meet interesting people to bond in love.

March

Your relationship may have reached a point of no return because of interpersonal differences and other issues. I see some difficult revelations and facts rising to the surface this month. You may realize that you, or your partner, are no longer committed to the relationship. However, you may be able to salvage the relationship by taking corrective measures. The fate of the relationship will depend on the male partner's efforts. I see an emotional time ahead when compassion, kindness and diplomacy will greatly help improve this relationship.

If you are looking for love, then it's time to relinquish archaic attitudes and idealistic notions of a lover.

April

I see you feeling more stable and in control of your love life. However, in the case of a relationship where problems and issues exist, this may be a crucial time to either make or break what you have in love. Mid-month, the situation will improve further and your relationship will enrich your life and give it deeper meaning. It is a good idea to consider a change of environment, such as a short break or holiday, to enhance your romance.

For the single Libra seeking love, there is good news in the offing this month. You may initiate a commitment and be ready to take the plunge in love.

May

You and your partner could be struggling with issues and interpersonal differences this month. Both of you may have to sit down with the intention to resolve these issues or part ways. A short break will be beneficial this month. This is not the time to cling to each other. Learn to give each other some space to think about what you both desire and what you can do to make this relationship work. Some amount of introspection will certainly help. You must reflect on your options and decisions.

If you are unattached, then you may receive some disappointing news. If you were hoping to make things work with a prospective lover, in all probability, you will discover that this relationship will not work out.

June

There will be mild conflict between you and your partner this month. Do not get into a conflict if it can be avoided, it may not be worth it. If your partner needs space, then it's best to give it to him/her. This will only help your relationship stabilize. You could be competing for your partner's attention this June. He/she may be involved with other issues and this may cause you some discomfort. The cards that I see depict a very loving and caring partner who is willing to reciprocate and satisfy your emotional needs. All you need to do is be patient and manage your love life gently and cautiously.

If you are single and wondering why your love life looks bleak then look within and stop feeling sorry for yourself and learn to love yourself before you expect someone else to love you.

July

Either you or your partner may cheat on the other. You must confront your partner and be honest with each other. This relationship may have reached a point of no return. I see that both of you have tried everything to salvage it but your efforts haven't been successful. Hence, a painful separation is likely this month. The month will end with a beautiful message. You must believe and hope in the good that lies beyond the difficult patch that you have been through this month.

If you are single and seeking love, then make time for love. I see you totally absorbed in your career which may not be giving you much time to explore options in love.

August

You and your lover may be finding it hard to make time for togetherness with other aspects of your lives encroaching into your relationship. Sit down and plan a schedule to fit love into it. I see that you are ready and eager to make a comeback in love and willing to give romance all the time and effort needed to make it successful. You have faith and a positive outlook which is all it takes to initiate a new beginning. I see that you are about to embark on one such beginning and may need to start from scratch.

The single Libra will be spoilt for choice with more than one suitor vying for his/her attention. However, this may lead to a lot of confusion. It's best to go slow, take your time and work things out gradually.

September

I see you enjoying several parties and celebrations involving you and your beloved. You should make the most of this fun phase since conflicts and arguments may arise later in the month. Ensure you express your point of view, but do so tactfully and lovingly. You will see victory and stability in love in the last few days of the month when your relationship will be harmonious and you will be in control of the situation.

The unattached Libra will find someone interesting and exciting at a marriage function or a similar event. This is the right place to network and find potential partners.

October

Your relationship may reach a point of stability this month and you could consider marriage or some other official arrangement. This may also mean taking a decision to live together. Some issue is likely to cause an imbalance in your love life as you move further into October. You will be torn between two aspects which are making life difficult for you. The earlier you make a choice and opt for the more favourable aspect for your love life, the better it will be for you.

The single Libra, who may be managing two potential lovers at a time, will face some confusion. This multitasking is difficult and it's best you choose the more favourable partner.

November

A woman will be part of your love scene this month. She could be an external influence like a mother, sister or a friend who is interfering more than needed. To ensure your relationship is smooth, you should keep this person's intervention to the bare minimum. Your relationship is all set to rise to new levels of contentment and stability. I see the card of the genie which depicts a wish. This wish, made in love, will be fulfilled this November.

If you are a single Libra, you will meet someone unusual and different from your image of a potential lover. This should be exciting. You will have to try something new to catch this person's eye.

December

In December, your relationship will have all the ingredients for success, will rise to greater heights of stability and happiness. Considering your differences and what you may have been through, a short break or a vacation is advised. This will only add to the happy climax and make you fall in love all over again. But do watch out for your tendency to dissect and analyse everything. Both overthinking and negative thinking are harmful for your relationship.

The single Libra will witness victory in love this December. You are about to get into a commitment with someone you have been dreaming about.

Health Forecasts

January

You may be battling emotional stress at the start of the year instead of making resolutions for your health. This emotional stress could be caused by repressed emotions such as anger and hatred towards someone or something. If this is the case, it's best that you let go of these negative emotions. The good news is that I see you gearing up to work on your health. If you are expecting test results, then they are likely to be good and you will be happy with them. If you have the tendency to overdo things, then you are advised to slow down.

February

You will recover from your ailment and your health will stabilize. You should consider going on a short break or a vacation that will refresh you and help you release all your emotional baggage. I see you stressed and worked up about something relating to your health or to other aspects of your life. If this is so, then know that worrying is not a solution. You should look at the bright side instead of focusing on the negatives. Don't let fear hinder your progress. Fight your greatest adversary, your mind, and stop its negative chatter. The month will end well and I see you getting ready to take on something new, such as an initiative or a venture of some sort. This will be exciting and promising. Keep your spirits up and continue to work on your health.

March

You will be initiating a new health regimen, routine or diet that will lead to positive results. This will be a challenge but you must work towards achieving your goals. If you start to lose hope because of lack of results, then remind yourself that you can achieve what you want. You will enter into this partnership with a new healer or a doctor. This association is going to be short-lived but it will guarantee results. You will be happy to have taken this step and will dedicate yourself to achieving a positive outcome.

April

You are enthused about taking on the health challenges that lie ahead. This energy that you exude is goal-oriented. Channelize it in the right direction and see the results that emerge. You should respect your body and work within its permissible limits. You will have to pay close attention to your body's needs and chart out a plan that includes regular exercise, a balanced diet and sufficient sleep.

The month will end with you reaping the rewards for your efforts. You may have put in a lot of hard work to achieve a certain fitness level, weight-loss, or weight-gain, in your quest to defeat an ailment, and now is the time to receive the returns.

May

The month will start off well. I see you making progress in your health and recovering from stubborn ailments which have troubled you for some time. A short break or a holiday will rejuvenate you. Mid-month, the news will not be so good. You may decide to terminate your association with a certain healer or doctor, or conclude some health regimen. The association may not have given you the expected results so there is no point in continuing it. The month will end well with your fitness levels and vitality back to normal.

June

You will experience defeat which will leave you feeling angry and upset. However, the longer you hold on to such emotions, the more problematic they will be for you. Instead, you should learn to deal with your emotions calmly and delicately. Look out for injuries and minor sprains this month. These may occur if you exercise or work recklessly. If you are already injured, then go slow. Any excessive stress on your body will cause a relapse of injury. I see a change coming your way this month. This change will set the course for a transformation. You may find it difficult to adapt to this change, but be assured that it will yield big rewards.

July

You are ready to work on your health and your overall sense of well-being so that you can eliminate your problems. You will be chalking out plans and strategies to eat right and exercise in moderation based on the needs of your body. This is the time to take quick action to be assured of immediate results. You have a health goal in mind and I see you working hard to achieve it. The month will end with some stress and worry. You may be dealing with a minor health issue but overthinking and spending too much time worrying about it may blow it out of proportion.

August

This month will start off very well and you will reap the rewards for your diligence. I see the influence of a health institution or a counsellor in your life. You could either meet a therapist or resort to meditation or some spiritual practice rendered by an institution. This approach will widen your horizons and help you deal with day-to-day issues. However, look out for some emotional upheaval which lies ahead. Your heart may suffer a blow and this could hamper your overall sense of well-being. Your well-being will eventually boil down to how you deal with the situation.

September

Chances are that you will be pushing yourself far more than needed this month. This could land you in trouble; so you should slow down and watch where you are headed. Take it easy and be mindful of the way you manage your body, mind and spirit. If you have been seeking a certain type of treatment, or looking for a good healer, doctor or a therapist, then this desire will be fulfilled this month. You will get what you always wanted for the betterment of your health.

October

You may decide to leave a comfortable position to pursue your dream. This difficult but imperative decision will cause you considerable stress and apprehension which can lead to health issues. Hence, it is important that you pay close attention to your mental well-being. The best way to deal with health issues is to look closely at your daily routine. Ask yourself if you get sufficient physical exercise, if your diet is balanced, if you are sleeping well, and if you take time out for meditation and other practices of this kind. If you can balance these aspects of your daily life, you will achieve positive health outcomes.

November

You will encounter a traditional healer who may adopt conservative practices to heal you. You may also turn to a counsellor or an institution that will get you back on your feet and help your health stabilize. However, mid-month, the situation may get out of hand causing you a lot of stress and worry. You may be feeling dejected and disappointed with the way your life has panned out. Getting angry, depressed or anxious will only make the situation worse. This is the time to take control and initiate new ways and means to achieve mental stability and physical betterment.

December

You will have to pay attention to various aspects of your health such as diet, rest, medication, therapy, exercise and mental well-being. Ensure you don't overdo anything or perform below par. Mid-month, you may face some emotional challenges and be thrown into a difficult state from which you may not be able to make a comeback. But you need to stay strong and hang in there. Watch your emotional quotient, calm yourself, believe in your potential and strength to fight back, and you will recover. The year will end in a few days and you will once again be at a crossroads, with many options to choose from. The confusion could be about choosing a doctor, a healer, a type of treatment or some medication. Weigh your options well and make an informed decision.

Wealth Forecasts

January

The year will start with a woman playing an important role in shaping your finances. Your finances look good at the start of January but there is scope for improvement and stability. You know what will work and how to go about doing it. Therefore, without further ado, take action to achieve your goals. Financial aid will be coming your way mid-month. Someone will decide to repay your kindness with a gift of money which will greatly boost your finances. At some stage, you may question your financial position. In my opinion, focusing on the positives of your life will help you find an answer to this question.

February

You may face a tight financial position this February and spend sleepless nights. Instead of brooding on your situation, consider corrective action to fix it. The good news is that you may soon reap the rewards for your hard work. You will see opportunities to make money which should lift your spirits up and help you get back on track. If your financial outcomes depend on someone else's decision, then you will see a move in the right direction.

March

If you need to take an important financial decision, do not procrastinate. Make an informed decision and do not merely skim the surface. If you have the tendency to splurge, then tighten your purse strings and watch where you are headed. If you have been working towards a certain financial goal, a promotion, a home or a car, then this wish will be granted mid-month.

April

A financial institution will play an important role in managing your finances this month. You may seek their expert advice or the advice of a person who will guide you in money matters. This will help you spend cautiously and plan your savings. It's good to play by the rules sometimes, and April is one such month for this. Do not be careless and block your money in stocks and bonds. Carefully study and research the avenues you want to consider for investment.

Some disappointing news is likely to come your way mid-month. One of your financial investments may have failed to yield the results you expected, leaving you dejected and disturbed. However, it's just a phase and it will pass. Your fortunes will take a turn for the better and I see a windfall on the cards. This money may come from a long-forgotten association, property, ancestral income or money from gambling or a lottery.

May

You may find yourself in a difficult situation because some financial decisions may have gone wrong or backfired. This will leave you with no choice but to terminate your association with that person, job or financial venture. Mid-month, you may receive an unexpected gift of money or something more valuable that will cheer you up. May will end beautifully with the wheel of fortune turning in your favour.

June

You may face a financial deficit at the start of the month which will bother you, especially since those around you will be enjoying abundance. If you need financial help, don't hesitate to ask. Despite the odds that you will be facing, I see an unexpected raise or a bonus coming your way. This may be hard to believe, but you will receive this before the end of the month. This will mark your recovery from the phase you were in at the beginning of the month.

July

You may worry more than is necessary about your finances this month. This anxiety originates from insecurity about money, and your experiences in the recent past could be hindering your progress in the present. If you have been working hard, then you will reap the rewards for your efforts. It is only a matter of time. In fact, you may see a favourable outcome this very month.

However, if you believe that you are not being fairly compensated, then this may be the time to speak up and bring about a change in your remuneration. The answers to your financial woes lie in your past. If you take a walk down memory lane you will realize that someone or something can help you deal with your finances and get you to where you would like to be.

August

You could be stuck in a job or a situation where your chances of survival look bleak. This may be a troublesome phase and you know that the only solution is to conclude the existing arrangement. As you choose to move away from this billet, you might experience significant financial stress. This is the right time to patiently enumerate your skills and talents and look for something that could change the game entirely. I see you discovering a creative skill which could set the ball rolling for you again. This may be a good time to use your innate talent to create more wealth avenues for yourself.

September

You may face a tight financial situation this month. The only way to change this is to share your wealth with those who are less fortunate. This will garner more for you. However, the charity should be purely altruistic, not avaricious. What matters is the spirit of giving. Ultimately, what goes around, comes around. By the end of the month, the good times will be back again. You will see financial opportunities and contracts coming your way. This will put you back in the game and help you rise up the ladder.

October

You may be overwhelmed by your financial obligations this October. Resources will be scarce but expenses will be many. Also, recent events may have rattled you. It's best to look at your situation dispassionately and work out solutions for permanent relief. Mid-month, you may begin to see the rewards for all your hard work. Avoid extravagance; prudence is the need of the hour.

The end of the month, however, may not be all that good. You may face a tight financial situation while you await your rewards. My advice to you is not to lose hope and not to get impatient. Your situation is about to change.

November

You will have sufficient money to consider the purchase of a car or a vehicle which has been on your mind for some time. You may also consider booking a long luxury holiday. This is good and is proof of how well your finances have turned out. There is some good news coming your way, mostly related to better work opportunities which will favour your finances. You could be considering a job change or a role change that promises better prospects. The month will end with a bonus, incentive or a raise.

December

There is hope and happiness for you as you close this year. Dame Fortune smiles upon you and you will have whatever you need to make your life comfortable and joyous. You could also consider taking some risks now, such as making big investments or selling something which is not moving as expected. Towards the end of the month, you will initiate a small venture or a partnership which promises prosperity and positive returns. This is good and will deliver the expected returns.

Career Forecasts

January

You will be enthused about taking up new challenges at the start of the year and be ready for what lies ahead. There is a need to be more disciplined, logical and organized in your approach. Working hard without discipline, logic and organization will have a negative impact on your productivity. Hence, you must get serious about the way you conduct your work and yourself. This is also the time when emotions will have to take a back seat. Think and act pragmatically rather than emotionally. You may be at a point when important decisions have to be taken so logic will be very useful. A very kind and compassionate man will support you in your work set-up.

February

A change is about to set in. You may decide to quit your existing job and move on. This may be due to your lack of interest in the existing job or because your passion is calling out to you to pursue happiness. It may be advisable for you to ask someone you know and trust for help. A woman who is fond of you and sees your true potential may come to your aid. You could also try and adopt a creative and passionate approach to your job. Respect and love what you do and your work will reciprocate.

March

March is a month when you will need to constantly remind yourself that the situation is going to change and there is room and hope for improvement. You need to stay positive and focused. You will start a venture or an initiative this month. This may be a short-term project or a partnership that could be a business, a freelance assignment or a joint venture of some sort which has sound potential. The results are guaranteed and this venture will be profitable.

April

If you are looking for employment, then it's about to come through. You could receive good news about an offer or an opportunity that matches your expectations. Do not hesitate to ask for what you deserve, and do so confidently. However, do remember that your employer may be monitoring you closely. This is not the time to slack off or get involved in any petty office politics. Play straight and hard and focus on winning hearts. Also watch your back since a certain amount of treachery and backstabbing will be taking place in the background. Be cautious when it comes to trusting and managing people.

May

You may decide to leave a job or terminate your association with your employer. You have done all you could to make this work for you, but your efforts may be futile. You are advised to wrap up the project, assignment, job or client relationship that fails to yield the expected results. Although this decision is going to give you sleepless nights, the problem is manageable and I see you bouncing back as you exit this month. You will receive some positive news of an opportunity or an offer which will open the doorway to many more opportunities.

June

If you are stuck in a dead-end job which is not right for you, then maybe you should consider moving on. In an existing work scenario, don't let your past rule your decisions in the present. Learn from your mistakes, make the necessary amendments and press on. A very authoritative and a determined man will be part of your work scene this month. He is someone you can trust, although he is rather judgemental. You are on the brink of completion, and now may not be the time to give up. Do not succumb to work pressure and stay committed to your deliverables. It is possible that you have been working too hard for too little pay. If this is the case, it's time you made your dissatisfaction known to people who can make a difference to your pay packet.

July

Your work will be looking good and moving smoothly at the start of this month. If you are awaiting a job opportunity, then in all probability it will come through. This may be an overseas posting or a break which could give you an international placement. However, do look out for conflicts and arguments at your workplace. There may be times when you have a heated argument with them. If you can calm down and let this stage pass, the situation will turn in your favour.

You will have reason to celebrate towards the end of the month. I see an office party or a reunion of some sort in which you will be actively involved.

August

If you are feeling trapped in a thankless job, but are staying on because of the security and regular pay cheque it provides, then now may be the time to take control of the situation and bring about a change. The answer to your greatest fears lies in your past. You may need to revisit it to discover someone who can connect you with an opportunity that you never thought about before. The month will end with some bitterness. I see you choosing to terminate an association or consider relocation in pursuit of your passion. Leaving a comfortable job and financial security is going to be a difficult decision, but in my opinion, it is the right thing to do.

September

If you are anticipating rewards for your efforts, then you may find that they will take a little longer to reach you. You will have to be patient. Don't let minor issues and other people's perspectives about your work pull you down. Someone may be working against you, but eventually your diligence will pay off. The people around you will finally realize your true potential. Channelize your energy in the right direction instead of wasting it on petty issues. You have a great deal to achieve; so stay focused and continue to do what you do best.

October

There is no point in worrying about your job. If you don't enjoy it, then you need to change the situation. Instead of brooding and procrastinating, turn your thoughts into action now. Your work will seem overwhelming mid-month, and you may find yourself sinking into despair and boredom. I suggest you use this time to keep your head down, beaver on and complete the task that has been assigned to you.

November

If you detest your job, then quit and find something exciting and challenging to do. But if you decide to stay on in your current situation out of fear of taking a risk or lack of security, then accept that this is your own choice. Mid-month, I see something interesting working out for you. This may emerge from your past. Look closely for clues in the form of people or things that can help you connect the dots and arrive at an answer which may very well change your career. The month will end with you taking the difficult decision to follow your dream and leave the comfort of your stable but boring job.

December

You will be getting ready to receive a promotion or a bonus, or settle into a new role or job. You will generally be in a happy state of mind with your work going smoothly and circumstances working out for you. You will be in for celebrations and parties later in the month, which will help you ease off from your busy schedule and enjoy your accomplishments. The year will end with you taking up a vocation or a role in which you will enthusiastically learn new skills and learn the ropes of the job, which will be exciting but challenging. You will be eager to take on what lies ahead, and will be ready to work hard and prove yourself. The year can't end on a better note than this.

SCORPIO

DEATH

Love Forecasts

January

January is a beautiful month and will start in a perfect way. I see you and your beloved involved in family functions. These functions or ceremonies may be your marriage or engagement that could take your love commitment to the next level. Enjoy this time and understand that a love commitment is a like a job. The more you work on it, the sweeter it will become.

The single Scorpio will spend too much time worrying about what lies ahead. You are concerned that you will remain alone. But you need to realize that these are just thoughts and not the reality.

February

You will be all set to work on your relationship and ready to deal with what comes next. A certain spark in you will motivate you to plan, strategize and be in complete control of your love life. You will be the one calling the shots and shaping the alliance in the manner you desire. But while you do this, remember not to encroach into your partner's space or create issues in your perfect romance: You can't force a person to accept your viewpoint.

The unattached Scorpio will be spoilt for choice. You have more than one option for a potential suitor.

March

I see you feeling hurt and disappointed with recent events. You may realize that your partner doesn't love or care for you. This will leave you feeling like you've been taken for a ride. However, in a relationship, both parties need to put in effort. Hence it is best that you sit down and talk out your differences, and find a middle ground. I see you deciding to end the relationship, or moving closer to its termination.

The month will end well and you could choose to leave this relationship or stay on. If you decide to stay on, then the relationship will begin to show improvement and maturity with time.

If you are seeking love, then you will meet someone very kind, compassionate and generous this month. This person is a giver and has a big heart.

April

It is quite possible that your ex-lover will appear out of the blue and leave a lasting impression on you. In such a situation, know where to draw the line. On the other hand, I see perfect harmony, respect, love and chemistry in your existing love life which will only grow stronger by the day. This is simply a miraculous time for romance, and you and your partner will be able to create magic in your life and strengthen your bond of love like never before.

The single Scorpio will be lost, bored and tired of seeking love. But before you point fingers at others or situations outside yourself, a period of introspection is prescribed to ask yourself if you are actually ready and willing to do the work to find a lover.

May

Your love relationship will see some happy times that will cheer you up. Mid-month, the situation may get heated and there is a possibility of a conflict. You may experience stress, tension and an emotional upheaval during this time. You could be feeling emotionally distraught and you may decide to take some impulsive decisions and pass hasty judgements. Treat your lover like a friend and offer him/her a chance to have a healthy discussion. Unfortunately, the relationship may not move in the direction you planned, and you and your partner may have to take some difficult decisions towards the end of the month.

The unattached Scorpio will be getting ready to fall in love and initiate a new committed relationship. This will lead you into an adventurous journey.

June

Your relationship will undergo a transition this month. You may have put in considerable effort to make it work but are yet to see the results. However, getting impatient and losing hope may not be the solution. Like everything else, it takes time for romance to evolve and mature. If you have been discussing issues and problems with your lover and he/she is simply not acting upon them, then it may be time to move on. Nevertheless, before you take a final decision, consult a counsellor or a friend. For all you know, a good counselling session may go a long way in resolving pent-up emotional problems and could stabilize the relationship.

If you are seeking love, then a potential partner may appear this month. This person is romantic, kind and emotional. You will have to adopt a gentle approach in dealing with him/her.

July

The more you try and hold on to an emotion, person or thing, the more it will slip away from you. Hence, it is best to let go when you need to. By acting clingy and possessive, you will be leaving little or no breathing space for your partner in this relationship. The male partner in this relationship is quite headstrong and opinionated. If you are the male partner, then you could be behaving in a manner which is not conducive to romance. However, if you are the female and your partner is a domineering male, then it would be best to let him have his space.

For the single Scorpio, the news may not be so good this month. You may have ended a relationship very recently and will be sceptical about getting into another one. Take your time and thoroughly evaluate your options before you reach a decision.

August

Your love life will be on an upswing with positive developments and good news emanating from other aspects of your life. All this will help you look at your love life in a positive light. There is a chance that conflicts may arise and shake the peace you have established. If you handle the situation tactfully, the differences may be avoided. The month will end on a happy note and I see you celebrating and rejoicing in love.

If you are seeking love, then look for it at marriage and engagement functions. Participate in such events and you have a good chance of meeting the perfect suitor.

September

You will manifest your greatest wish in love this September. If you have been looking for a commitment such as marriage or an engagement, then it will materialize. I see you euphoric after your greatest wish is fulfilled. However, there is a need to balance your work and personal life. Furthermore, a senior person, who is much older than you, will play an important role in shaping your relationship this month. In all probability, you will be drawn to this person. I see you excited about initiating a new adventure in love which you have never done before. But this may be outside your committed relationship and has its own risks.

The single Scorpio will be immensely attracted to a woman who is beyond his reach. This attraction has sexual undertones and is thrilling in its own way.

October

There will be love and compatibility with perfect harmony and balance between you and your partner, and both of you will be totally in love and looking out for each other. In my opinion, it is important for a relationship to be equal and well balanced. Hence, if you find your relationship becoming lopsided at any point in time, express your concerns and discuss these issues with your partner.

The unattached Scorpio will have to go beyond his/her usual haunts to find someone interesting and intellectually stimulating. It would be best to search for love in new and unexplored locales.

November

Conflicts, arguments and differences of opinions will arise in your relationship this month. You will have to watch your step with your better half. Go slow, don't intrude into your partner's space and try to be as calm as possible. It is good to express your point of view but do so gently. Acting clingy, desperate and possessive, all signs of weakness, will only make your partner feel suffocated. Sadly, I see this relationship failing. You may realize that the person you loved so much never really cared about you. You may choose to continue in this relationship while accepting this ugly truth, or let go entirely and move on.

If you are single and seeking love, then this may not be the right time for you. You will have to take a break from everything you are doing to consider your choices in love.

December

You could be struggling with repressed emotions of remorse, guilt and anger. During the month though a happy event like marriage, childbirth or something similar will stir positive emotions and help you manage the difficulties you faced initially. These are all happy beginnings in which the past hardly has any place. If you do decide to take a walk down memory lane, focus on positive memories. Do not let the past influence your present. There is a good possibility that your former partner will show up towards the end of December. This may cause the situation to get out of control, and hence tackle it carefully.

The single Scorpio will fall in love with someone who has always been part of your life this December. You may have never really seen this person in the light of love, but it is better late than never.

Health Forecasts

January

You have probably made your own list of health resolutions, but you may have little or no time to work on them. Your career is likely to eat into all the time you have allocated for your health. You will face constant stress and work pressure and will be feeling overwhelmed. But since you can't turn down the work you have already accepted, you can try and reduce your work stress. A deep-seated emotion of remorse associated with your past will have an impact on your health. You should learn to be mindful about the present and let go of the emotional baggage that is holding you back. A kind, generous and compassionate man will enter your health scene towards the end of the month. He will be a healer, a family member or a friend whose presence itself will be uplifting.

February

You will have a fresh start as you leave the stress and tension of the previous month behind. A short break or a vacation of even two days will bring in huge respite; so consider getting out and rejuvenating. Look out for what is coming your way mid-month. Some minor health issue may crop up, but you will be pressed for time and short of money to take a closer look at it. However, it would be a good idea to get to the bottom of the problem and eradicate the issue from its root. The month will end well with you initiating a partnership with a person who could be a health instructor, a healer or someone who can bring about positive developments in your health.

March

A woman will help you recover this month. She is compassionate and helpful. This is also the time when love and creativity will heal old wounds. If you have been trying to have a child, then the news is positive and will alleviate most of your mental stress. There could also be some progress in your financial and personal life, with marriage and other important events lifting your spirits and putting you in a happy space. However, the month will end with some amount of confusion because you will have to choose one option from many. This choice will be related to your health, particularly therapies or treatment procedures, and doctors.

April

If you have been suffering from poor health, then your condition is about to take a turn for the better. Your life in general will be on an upswing which will reflect positively on your health. A man, who could be a doctor or a healer, will step into your health scene this month. He has knowledge and understanding of the ailment you are suffering from. He will be useful in this situation. However, if you have doubts about his diagnosis, get a second opinion. This will allay your doubts.

May

If you are expecting some test results, then the news is likely to be positive. You will be relieved and overjoyed about the outcome. But do not slack off because of the change that may come along mid-month. You may have to adjust and adapt to what life throws at you. This new development will give you an opportunity to transform your life. You may have to bring about important lifestyle alterations and commit to a health routine that involves regular physical exercise.

June

June will start off beautifully with good news, positive outcomes, joyous celebrations and reunions. Your health will do well, and due to positive outcomes from other factors of life, you will be in a happy state of mind. You have put up a brave fight and recovered from all the deficits you faced so far. The month will end with some amount of confusion. Something will be bothering you about your health, but the answers will be hazy. If you have a doubt, then thoroughly investigate your health issue until you are convinced.

July

You will be enthused to take up a new health initiative this month. This initiative may be a new diet, exercise routine, treatment, etc. However, you will have to try various permutations and combinations to see what works best for your body and mind. Tempering these elements will not be easy considering your present lifestyle. Moderation is the key to success. The right balance will help achieve the best possible outcome.

The month will end on a pleasant note. I see you receiving positive news, and any expected outcomes will turn out to be good.

August

You will have to watch where you are headed with your exercise regimen and other physical activities this month. Avoid injuries and go as slow as possible on new health routines. If you have sustained an injury, then you must be gentle on yourself. The results will come in due course, and patience will only make them sweeter. A kind and considerate woman will help you recover from your present health condition. You could also look for creative ways to work on your recovery and overall sense of well-being. The month will end with a situation that will make you feel emotionally burnt out. Instead of looking at this limitation negatively, look at it as a breather for your body. Use this time to recover.

September

You may be finding it difficult to get solutions to your health problems. Your lack of progress in this regard may be bothering you. Instead of pushing yourself and getting stressed out, my suggestion is to take a break, relax and change your perspective. This may help you come up with a different approach. Do not take the first pronouncement about your health as your only option. If you doubt it, then it's best that you seek another opinion. The end of the month will be a challenging period. Your health condition could be the result of past repressed emotions. You are troubled within and have probably overlooked this aspect of your life. It's best to face these emotions, deal with them and end your association with the past. You could also consider meditation and deep breathing.

October

Go back in time and take a walk down memory lane to figure out why you feel the way you do. These issues could be related to your childhood experiences, and you will need to resolve them to move forward.

There could be problems related to your health mid-month. If you are expecting test results, then don't get too worked up about them. Your health issues could be the result of miscommunication with your body. Listen carefully and heed your body's needs.

November

There is someone who may repay your past act of kindness. This may be in the form of financial aid. Accept this as it will help you deal with your health issues. A little further into the month and your health may begin to deteriorate. You will need to watch where you are headed emotionally once again. You will also face other stressors associated with your love and professional life, and may come upon certain revelations that will leave you disappointed and hurt. However, this disheartening phase will be overcome as you reap the rewards for your efforts. Your health will recover as you approach the end of the month and you will begin to receive the outcomes you had envisioned at the beginning of the year.

December

Although you will be at your fittest at the start of this month, you will have to deal with some difficult times mid-month when your repressed emotions will surface. These feelings of guilt, remorse or regret seem to have been the hallmark of this year. You may have to seriously consider a session with a counsellor to help deal with the emotional baggage which has been weighing you down since your childhood. The year will end in a way that I had not expected. The last few days of the month will see you battling anxiety, stress and tensions caused by your hectic and stressful professional life. You should strike a balance between your personal and professional lives and learn to say no when needed; otherwise you may ruin all the progress you have made in your health.

Wealth Forecasts

January

You will receive some good news about your finances at the start of the year which will open new opportunities for you that will lead to greater wealth. Your investments will perform well, real estate will be soaring and you will generally receive money one way or the other. You will manifest some life-changing opportunities in wealth early in the year. If your financial outcomes are dependent on someone else's decisions, then the news will be good.

February

You will need to watch where you are putting your money. If you have doubts about any financial or investment avenue, then thoroughly research the project and ensure there is no room for misgivings. This is a good time to follow your intuition which will guide you in the right direction. Your recovery will begin from here and you will see small cash inflows which will be enough to tide your over your difficulties. I see perfect balance in your income and expenditure.

March

Your wealth will be on an upswing and circumstances will favour you. If you are involved in a business, then it is likely to generate considerable profit this month. You should use this money prudently and allocate it to important expenditure or investments. Even though your financial situation may be going well, you may be feeling incredulity about your sudden progress. Thus, it is important to shed these insecurities related to money. They will not do you any good. The end of the month will find you on the horns of a dilemma between two options, unable to determine which avenue is more profitable. If you want to take a viable decision, do back it up with sound research and expert guidance.

April

This month, you may receive financial aid as repayment for your good karmic deeds in the past, or you may donate money to someone who is in need. In either case, you will benefit. If you have applied for a business loan, then it is likely to come through this April. A little further into the month, you may begin to cavil at your present financial condition and forget to consider all those wonderful blessings that the universe has showered upon you. A woman will play an important role in shaping your finances towards the end of April. She could be an expert who will help you understand your position and plan accordingly.

May

You will make some big-ticket purchases such as a car or some other vehicle, or you may plan a holiday. You will generally be feeling happy with recent developments, and your stocks, shares and other investments will generate positive returns. Mid-month, you are likely to receive some positive news which will motivate you to surge ahead. If your finances depend on someone else's decision, then this will work in your favour.

June

You will be in a predicament, finding it impossible to take a decision with the array of options available. These financial avenues may well be tempting, but go slow and make the right choice. By mid-month, money will flow in more easily and you will have enough to spend and to save. Remember to share your wealth with the needy. The more you give, the more you will receive. The month will end on a fabulous note. I see the card of the genie which implies that your greatest wish in terms of wealth will be fulfilled.

July

You will be doing too many things with too few resources. This imbalance especially pertains to two elements which may be pulling you in different directions. You cannot continue to work like this with two projects, or two kinds of investment plans, or manage both a business and a service. You will be compelled to make a choice between the two. Avoid making any big financial leaps at this time.

You will be ready to embark on something exciting and new in the middle of the month. You will receive a big bonus, a hefty pay hike, an incentive or money in some other form at the end of the month. You will suddenly find yourself cash rich. This is a wonderful time for you.

August

After the events of July, you will be euphoric. You have many reasons to be happy, one of which is the feeling of being prosperous. A little further into the month and you may create imbalance in your wealth once again, with your expenses exceeding your income. You may suddenly decide to make a big-ticket purchase, which is ill-advised at this time. you will need to amend your attitude as well as the way you manage your finances.

September

This is a good time to invest as long as you play by the rules. You will have to start small and consider the expert opinions of advisers, bankers or other professionals before you choose the best possible option for investment. A conservative approach and investing in a small scheme may be ideal. If you are expecting a new round of job offers, business portfolios, or wealth opportunities, then you may be disappointed. This may take longer than expected. In the last few days of the month, I see you attaining some sort of completion in your financial goals. This is also the right time to ask for a raise if you feel you deserve it.

October

You are probably feeling defeated and lost because you believed that your work would lead to greater possibilities. All you can do now is to hang in there and not lose hope. If you are considering the option of taking a major leap in investments, perform due diligence first. Mid-month, the situation will take an ugly turn. You may find that your investments have hit rock bottom; your job could be at stake; and your stocks may have turned to dust. You may have to prepare yourself for the financial challenges that lie ahead. All that is in your power is to adapt to the change and accept what comes your way.

November

Money may be tight and you will have to manage your life with limited resources. Do not take a wrong decision that will land you in trouble. Use your money prudently and allocate it to the right uses. Even if your money situation improves, spending unnecessarily is not warranted. You must go slow and budget your spending. The month will end with small returns trickling in. You may choose to start a new job, an alternative career or take up something that leads to some extra money. Even if this amount is small, it will make a huge difference to you in your current situation.

December

You may decide to spend some money on renovating your home or your office space to add some comfort and luxury to your life. This is good as long as you keep the mortgage small and limit your expenditure. Take a loan only if you can comfortably repay it. There could be a slight imbalance in your expenditure and income this month; so you may have to avoid large purchases. The year is about to end and I see a happy closure for you. You have peace, happiness and stability which leads me to believe that you have everything you need for a comfortable life.

Career Forecasts

January

When someone criticizes you in your field of work, you are likely to defend yourself. You will be attacked in this way at the start of the year when I see you facing deceit and treachery. You will realize that people can't be trusted easily and that you have to watch your back. Work politics may take an ugly turn. If you are losing hope and the future seems bleak, weather this storm and don't give up. Even if you are trapped in the same job for ten years, there is always hope of a positive outcome. Keep looking for a good opportunity and grab it when it comes. You may receive some negative news at the end of the month. It is quite possible that you may lose your job, project, assignment or position. Although this has been brewing for some time, it has only surfaced now.

February

You will be rewarded for your efforts and the hard work you have put in so far. If you are looking for a job, then it is about to come through with just the right pay and role for you. The month will end with you taking on a new initiative. This may be a partnership or a joint venture involving you and someone else. This partnership has good scope and from where I see it, positive results are guaranteed. You will greatly benefit from this association although this venture may not last longer than six to twelve months.

March

You will be in a state of total chaos and imbalance. Therefore, in order to achieve success and calm, you will have to temper the opposing elements with care and strike the right balance. These opposing elements could be two bosses, two jobs, two colleagues or two types of projects. A woman will play an important role in shaping your career. Her composure will greatly help you cope with the pressure and the difficult situations. In general, you should try to adopt a creative approach to your problems. Towards the end of March, you may find a teacher or a mentor who can guide you through your problems. His guidance will stabilize your work and help you manage it in the right way.

April

Mild conflicts and issues will arise at your workplace; so be careful about the way you handle people and don't be too pushy. A tactful approach will go a long way in helping you manage people better. If you are looking for a job, then humility is the key to getting one. You will make progress in your career this month provided you drop out of the old school and adapt to the new ways and techniques of working. You may be awaiting some news related to your work, such as a job offer, a project or an assignment. But there is some delay in this and your wait may get extended.

May

If you are stuck in a dead-end job where you don't receive any appreciation and where the environment isn't healthy for you, then now may be the time to take a decision to resign. If the work is too much for you, do not hesitate to ask for help. You will receive rewards and appreciation for your hard work, and you deserve every bit of this success. These rewards may be in the form of a pay hike or an incentive. The month, however, will end with some amount of worry and tension regarding job security and I see you spending sleepless nights towards the end of May.

June

A very strong, authoritative man will be part of your work scene this June. He could be your direct boss or a senior who will be supportive and willing to help you. You are keen to take on the new adventure that awaits you along with its risks. This could be a new project, an assignment or a job. You will receive an offer with a hefty pay packet or you could be appraised rather positively in your existing set-up. This is also the time when people will be looking up to you.

July

You will accomplish all your goals, targets, tasks or deliverables this month. You have been working very hard and success is guaranteed. However, if you feel that you are underpaid, then this may be the right time to flag it up. Your past will play an important role in your career this July. Something or someone will emerge from your past and rekindle old connections. These connections will help you answer some important questions in your career. If you are looking for a change, then it will come soon. You will probably decide to leave your job to follow your heart. This may seem a bit cataclysmic, but trust your instincts and know that the universe will guide you in the right direction.

August

You will be doing exceptionally well and will feel happy and emotionally stable. You will find everything that you have been seeking in your career this month. All your impossible projects or difficulties will be overcome and you will rejoice over your success. People will look up to you and this will only boost your confidence. I see you celebrating and embracing all the attention and appreciation coming your way. The month, however, will end with a few unforeseen defeats and failures. Do look out for difficult bosses and peers who may discredit or disregard your work.

September

You can expect a change both in terms of your job and your salary. This will be wonderful for you. If you are looking for a job, then there is a good chance that you will attract something good to yourself this September. You could be stuck in a place where the work has become monotonous. What you need to do is to take some time off and reflect on what your options are. Deep introspection may just help you find the solution to this problem within yourself.

October

Your employer will be closely monitoring your work this October. So be extra careful since even a minor mistake may get you into trouble. This is not the time to be involved in office politics as there could be instances when you are deceived or stabbed in the back. Be cautious about whom you trust and how much information you share. You may be inundated and overwhelmed with the volume of work. This is a good time to ask for help. However, stay away from conflicts and arguments. The situation could get heated if you don't deal with it in time.

November

Your work will go very well and because of your hard work, you will be virtually indispensable in your place of work. However, this doesn't mean that you should get complacent and start slacking off. You may have to win over a man who is part for your work scene. He could be your immediate boss or a senior. The end of the month may be a stressful period with tensions arising at your workplace. You may face conflicts and heated arguments which can land you in trouble. Don't take things personally and don't let people and their judgements impact you negatively.

December

The month will start well and I see you enjoying a strong position and success in your work. There won't be a better time than this to move on and take up something more exciting. Look at what awaits you on the other side if you take the risk and change jobs this December. You will have to make a choice between staying in your comfort zone or taking up a new job and embarking on an adventure of a lifetime.

SAGITTARIUS

TEMPERANCE

Love Forecasts

January

You are bored in your existing relationship because you believe it has lost its spark. You may wonder why this has happened. However, before pointing fingers at your partner, you should consider what you are contributing to this relationship. There is hope for your relationship as long as you are willing to work on it. It is best that you and your partner sit down and sort out your differences before it is too late and the passage of time has wreaked irrevocable damage.

The single Sagittarius will be competing for the attention of a potential suitor or others are chasing you for your attention. In case of the former, the competition is stiff and if it's the latter, you need to choose wisely.

February

You and your partner will be stuck in conflicts and issues which could take place due to other aspects of your life. You may have to look at your contribution to this relationship. As you move closer to the end of the month, you may be tempted to fight or argue in the heat of the moment. You may feel that your partner does not share your feelings, which will be disheartening and painful to accept initially. You may want to give up the relationship. But hold on, keep that temper in check. You may be making a mistake and jumping to conclusions.

The unattached Sagittarius will try hard to moderate all the elements of his/her life to make time for love. If you are caught up in an unbalanced situation, try to balance your life before you move ahead in your quest for love.

March

You could consider getting into a commitment, a live-in arrangement or even marriage. This journey will be new for you and will have its share of excitement and danger. But I see you exhilarated about this new adventure and I pray you enjoy every bit of it. If you have been feeling disappointed or tired about the way your relationship is progressing, the situation will improve mid-March. You will have the right balance and the happiness which you desire in your love life. A change in attitude and approach will go a long way in helping you deal with the normal issues faced in love. If you can work on your ego tantrums, anger issues and emotional dependency, you will be able to restore the peace and love in your ongoing relationship.

The unattached Sagittarius will be spoilt for choice. There will be many suitors to pick from. Who will be the right one is a million-dollar question. You may have to study their backgrounds well, do thorough research and then make an informed choice.

April

Although you will be considerate and gentle and will put in the effort needed to keep this relationship going, arguments may arise and lead to serious conflict. You will have to be tactful in dealing with your partner and consider giving him/her some space. This will be most crucial at this juncture. Mid-month, you will regret something about the past which will have an influence on your relationship in the present. You may give up on the relationship altogether and consider ending it. Look at this end as a catalyst for a brand-new beginning in the future.

The single Sagittarius will be swept off their feet by someone attractive and impressive. You should be ready for the excitement that awaits you.

May

I see the card of marriage, engagement or the news of childbirth. I see you and your partner totally in love and ready for a new beginning. It is important to express your point of view firmly before you are taken for granted. While discussing your areas of concern, it is best to exercise caution and handle your partner with care. There is hope for improvement and I see you happy and motivated in love. I also see that this relationship has a strong life line and, whatever happens to it, you two will stay strong.

If you are seeking love, then a kind, generous and compassionate person will come along this May. This opportunity will need a thorough evaluation. You must consider giving it your best shot.

June

June is going to be a challenging month for your relationship. You may face difficulties in your relationship or it will be on its last legs because of the failure of your efforts to save it. Now both you and your partner will have the opportunity to start afresh and move on if that is what is mutually decided.

The single Sagittarius will meet an enchanting and headstrong woman. She could be someone who keeps you on your toes.

July

There can be no better time for love than this. A change of scene will be a huge help and you should consider taking a short break with your beloved to rejuvenate. This will give you quality time together and will help you get some clarity of thought. You have come a long way with your partner and may be expecting a serious commitment now. You will have to be patient. The best way to get your partner to agree to your terms will be to strategize. Act distracted and I am sure he/she will be ready for a commitment.

If you seek true love, then this month will be interesting. You will be vying for someone's attention or you may have many suitors trying to get your attention.

August

Something is not right about your relationship this month. You will be in a predicament and seeking answers to several questions. Instead of looking out, you must consider looking within. A small break alone (perhaps even a long walk) could help clear the air and give you some answers. A romance from the past may be rekindled this month. You will be in a dilemma between two options or two aspects of your life. Handling both at a time will be impossible, and you may have to let go of one of them. This will help restore the missing balance and peace in your love life. If you are still unhappy, then now may be the time to decide if you want to be in this relationship or let it go.

The single Sagittarius will be involved with too many things to have time for love. To find love, one must make time.

September

September is a good month for your love relationship which will rise to new heights. A little further into the month and I see your work taking its toll on your relationship. If this is so, then know where to draw the line and balance your work and personal life. You will have to make time for your relationship despite your work pressure. The month will end with your partner raising a valid question: Are you doing your duty in the partnership? Your contribution may be dwindling and these questions are likely to arise. Look into the matter before it is too late to fix it.

If you are unattached, then this month will bring some good news. You are about to start something new in matters of the heart.

October

This is a competitive phase for your love relationship. Even though you are in a relationship, you may have others interested in you and giving you a lot of attention. The key to a successful life lies in balance. You may have to balance all the aspects of your life such as work, health, wealth and love in order to establish synergy.

Moderation is an important element here. The end of the month may not be such a great time for your love life. You may realize that the person you deeply care for doesn't feel the same way about you. This may be disheartening and you may feel left out and let down.

The unattached Sagittarius must learn self-love first. If you do not appreciate yourself, how can you expect someone else to love you?

November

A woman will greatly influence your love life this month. She is not your lover and her influence will not be that positive. In my opinion, you should keep her intervention to the minimum. The man in this relationship is strong, opinionated, domineering and inflexible. His attitude can cause friction in the relationship. If your partner is such a man, then protect your emotional side and be assertive when you deal with him. If you are the man in this relationship, then know your partner feels threatened by your attitude, which is not a healthy sign.

The unattached Sagittarius will meet someone kind and generous this month. This person is loving and very approachable.

December

This month looks positive with your relationship growing and maturing into a strong bond of love. You will reap the rewards for your efforts when you get love and respect in return. You will also have a transformed approach towards life and love because of what you have learnt this year. The woman in this relationship has played a very important role in securing a strong bond. She has been gentle, persistent and loving, and the success of the relationship can be attributed to her efforts.

The single Sagittarius will have to put in some effort to find the right match. You must get out and mingle. Staying in the background won't help. Get out and be seen by potential suitors.

Health Forecasts

January

Your health will look good at the start of the year. There is balance and harmony in your body, which is reflected in the way you conduct yourself and carry out your tasks. This month, your primary focus will be on establishing a new arrangement for your well-being, such as some kind of partnership with a healer or a health or fitness instructor. In the last few days you will manifest one of your greatest wishes in health. This may mean a certain treatment or a goal which is important for your overall sense of well-being.

February

You will conquer your ailments or achieve the health goals you had set for yourself this month. But your health will begin to deteriorate as the month progresses. You may experience a lot of emotional upheaval during this time. These stressors may cause unnecessary anxiety and panic attacks. You must calm down and address the situation gently and calmly. If your doctor or healer has made a diagnosis and you feel a second opinion is needed, then go ahead and get it. The end of the month will be a better time when you will be gearing up for some important emotional developments.

March

You are very goal-oriented, ready to take on any health challenge. I see you at your fittest doing all the things you want to do for your health. You will be feeling energized and totally renewed. This is a wonderful state to be in.

But do be careful about how you conduct yourself at work. You could be feeling overwhelmed with the excessive work pressure and stress. A good night's sleep, a nutritious diet and regular exercise will go a long way in promoting good health.

April

A woman will play an important role in your life this month. If you have the tendency to repress your emotions, then change this attitude and face them. The month will end well and you will be happy about the way you have managed your health so far – eating right, getting enough exercise and managing your emotions. This is the best way to attain a healthy body and mind. You will be rejoicing and celebrating your achievements in health with parties, reunions and get-togethers.

May

You may be insecure, apprehensive or stressed out about certain situations which are not in your control. Meditation will help you deal with all your troubles and see them with a fresh perspective. A change is coming your way and adapting to it is not going to be easy. In fact, it may adversely affect your emotional health. Mid-month, you could go through a major imbalance when you will have no control over what is about to unfold. What you can do is to take care of the three elements of your being – your body, mind and soul.

June

You will begin to make progress in your health in June. If you are suffering from a chronic ailment, then ponder about what caused it. Your aches and pains may be the result of repressed emotions or excessive rumination related to the past. This needs to be addressed. You will find the solution to your problem when you spend some time in introspecting on the root cause of the issue. The month will end with some good news if you are planning to have a baby. You are likely to conceive this month. If this is not something you want or planned for, then you may want to take precautions now.

July

Your health will finally begin to improve this month and I see you resuming your old health routine and eating right, resting well and working on your body as before. During the middle of the month, you should focus on adopting a compassionate and loving approach towards life. This will help you heal. You will meet a healer, an experienced man who is compassionate and kind. He will know his work well and will help you heal your ailment. You will have to follow his advice. He has rigid views but he will be useful to you.

August

You have worked very hard to get to where you are in terms of health and because of these efforts, you will see an improvement in your ailments and your fitness goals being met. However, you will need to continue to maintain a balanced lifestyle instead of getting carried away by your success and becoming lax in your health efforts. Towards the end of the month, I see that your health may decline. If you have misgivings about your doctor's or healer's treatment, then act on it and seek a second opinion.

September

There will be a certain imbalance in your life because you will be dealing with two opposing elements of your health or two aspects of your life simultaneously. This imbalance needs to be corrected before it begins to take its toll on your health. Mid-month, I see you taking control of your health. You will begin to make progress and stabilize emotionally. A kind and compassionate woman will help you heal. She could be your spouse, mother, friend or a healer of some sort who has a soft and feminine touch. Her care and love will help you heal from all the physical and emotional deficits of your life.

October

You may have to pay close attention to what your body is trying to communicate to you. If you have been suffering from aches and pains, then you need to slow down, heed your body's protest and accept its limitations. Mid-month will be a great time for your overall recovery. I see you taking a break, a short holiday which will revitalize you and provide a much-needed change. The month will end very well and I see you feeling good and fit after a long period of dealing with health issues.

November

Your recovery has begun and you will see positive outcomes in November. The dark hiatus is over and from here onwards you can look forward to a bright phase. However, you must watch your health regimen. Stay away from injuries and exercise extreme caution. If you are already injured, then go slow. While you are recovering, continue to perform your health routine in moderation.

December

You will start this month on a very positive note and I see you initiating a new journey into a specific health routine. This is more on the lines of a venture with someone for the betterment of your health. You have all that is needed – courage, determination and discipline – to make this venture a success. Any health problems arising now will be caused by repressed emotions. Hence, you need to resolve your emotional issues either by letting them go or facing them. The key to success is doing everything in moderation. Don't overdo anything or perform below par on any given task. A well-balanced life, with all actions in moderation, will render positive results.

Wealth Forecasts

January

Your decisions in the present are being influenced by what has gone by. You need to let go of this remorse and focus on the present which has so much potential to generate wealth. You will take up a new vocation, course or a job which promises good returns. There will be plenty of reasons to feel happy towards the end of the month. You will have money coming in more easily now and your life will be comfortable.

February

You could go through a phase where your finances are at an all-time low. Money will be moving very slowly towards you and the delay in receiving funds will leave you in the doldrums. While everyone else will be enjoying a state of abundance, you will be feeling left out and let down. But all this will change if you hang on and stay patient. Mid-month, your finances should improve and there will be enough to take care of you and your family. Your investments might suffer a beating towards the end of the month. You will be worried about the change in scenario but there is very little you can do about it.

March

Your financial situation will be better than what it was last month. But this may not be the time to take any hasty decisions or make big purchases. You may be considering a new avenue for investment or a medium that can generate greater wealth opportunities. I see you eager and thrilled to initiate this change which may be related to your career. The month will end beautifully with a sudden turn of events. You may be granted a hefty bonus, an increment or an offer which will open a portal to greater possibilities in wealth.

April

You will be able to use your money to pamper yourself which means visiting spas and retreats or taking a short break to experience luxury and the power of money. You will also be able to save a major portion of your income. This is a great comeback from the way the year started. An old contact may emerge from your past, and this connection will lead to an opportunity to generate more money that you may not have thought possible before. Your answer to your financial woes lies in the past.

May

If you are eagerly awaiting returns on your investments or any other financial gains, then let me inform you that this will get delayed. Your money will come but in its own sweet time. The more impatient you get, the more you will move away from this wealth. Also watch where you invest your money. Avoid any big leaps and maintain your liquidity. If you are approached for a loan, you may have to turn the request down. I am saying this because the chances of your loan being repaid are remote. Taking the expert opinion of bankers, financial advisers or planners will help you formulate a good action plan for investing your money.

June

The month will start well with money flowing in and you will have enough to take care of your expenses. You could consider sharing your money with those who don't have it. This way you will get back what you give. By the time you reach the end of the month, these worries and tensions will begin to overwhelm you. Your money may begin to slip away and you will be worried about meeting your basic expenses. Use creative ideas to overcome the problem you are in now.

July

Wealth will begin to flow in so you can rest and take it easy. However, use restraint in your spending and put your money to good use. You should try and save as much as you can for any unforeseen contingencies. A woman will play an important role in shaping your finances. She is very good with financial planning and you could learn a lot from her. You need to manage your insecurities regarding money calmly and patiently. Please work on turning such pessimism into optimism before they begin to attract negative outcomes in reality. Simply give more to get more!

August

Whatever you wish for financially will come to pass. This is great and you must put this money to good use. But while the situation looks good now, if you have the tendency to worry and brood over your financial status going awry, then such a thought may just become a self-fulfilling prophecy. You may end the month in a less than positive way. You may begin to feel the pinch of a deficit of money and be in the doldrums. But the situation is not all bad and if you deploy your mind and skills to finding a solution to your problem; you may very well succeed in doing so. If you want millions then think like a millionaire.

September

You may be surprised when you receive rewards for your hard work. There may not be any signs to presage such a windfall, but trust me it will come. However, what you need to watch are your thoughts. You need to stay calm and avoid getting worried about your finances. The month will end with an exciting discovery. During the difficult times, you may discover a talent or a skill which will help you earn more money. This could become an alternative source of income and has great potential.

October

The fear of losing a regular salary and a sense of security will tie you down to a dead-end job. In my opinion, if you are unhappy don't let the fear of losing a regular pay cheque keep you stuck in a rut. Break free and follow your heart. The good news is that I see you pursuing what you love in the middle of the month. You may come upon your dream job or a passion-turned-into-a-profession kind of set-up which will open doors to many opportunities. Someone may not be entirely honest with you about a financial decision you are about to take. If you have even a fraction of doubt about the investment, get to the bottom of it and investigate everything in detail.

November

The opportunities or returns that you are expecting will be delayed; it is best to stay calm and patiently wait for these to come along. This is the time to avoid extravagance and keep track of where your money is going. The good news is that despite the odds, your financial situation is about to change. You will witness a path-breaking opportunity that will pave the way for money to flow in.

December

You may get some positive news as the year draws to a close. But while you may be getting ready to receive the money which is coming to you, you may have to accept that this money will not be sufficient to meet all your financial obligations. You may have to prioritize the more important ones. Best way to deal with this phase is to stay positive. You are in for some happy times ahead and should ignore the niggling issues that you may face in the last days of this month.

Career Forecasts

January

Your career will start very well in the new year. You may have received a hefty pay cheque, an unexpected bonus or a good raise in your salary. Further into the month, you will enjoy a lot of power and attention in your workplace. You will be at your best this month and enjoy all the glory and success that will come along with your raise and greater responsibility. Towards the end of the month, you may decide to quit on a high note or simply take a short break. If you decide to quit, then it will be with the intention to follow your heart. But if you decide to take a short break, it will be to rest and rejuvenate before taking up something new that could be both challenging and exhilarating.

February

You will be brimming with fabulous ideas and interesting concepts this month. You are considering channelizing these ideas into reality and are enthused to take on what you believe will effect a change. But while doing so, do not appear too aggressive and pushy. Handle people around you diplomatically and package your ideas and concepts in a way that will be acceptable to everyone. I see victory in the middle of the month. You will succeed in the first few weeks and whatever you have thought and incorporated will serve you well. There is perfect balance in your work. If you are seeking a new job or an alternative offer, then one such opportunity, an overseas one, is on its way to you.

March

March is going to be a tricky month and you may have to watch where you are headed with office politics. There will be occasions when you will find yourself embroiled in conflicts. It's best to handle things tactfully and express your viewpoint assertively, not aggressively. If you are looking for work, now is the time to present yourself with utmost humility. You could be dealing with two projects or two people, and the decision to pick one may be taken out of your hands. You may have to be firm and choose the option or the side which you feel is more favourable to you.

April

You could be asked to move on or shift into another role which may seem impossible to deal with. But this transition will set the course for new opportunities which would normally have not come your way. You will now be compelled to leave the security of a comfortable but thankless job for a new beginning. You may regret this and cry over what has occurred, but brooding over it won't help.

The end of the month will bring forth some positive news. You will begin to make a breakthrough with a new job placement or work opportunity. It is wonderful that you have managed to make a comeback so quickly.

May

Your work is being closely monitored so now is the time to excel in it. In case you have been slacking off, get serious, otherwise you could find yourself in hot water. Also avoid jumping to conclusions and taking hasty decisions. You may face some stress in dealing with difficult people, or find that your seniors or peers are working against you. The month will not end well. You may be overwhelmed with what is happening and teetering on the brink of calling it quits.

However, it may be too late to do this now; instead, if you hang on a little longer, you will see victory.

June

There is nothing that you can't accomplish this month. But if you feel that you deserve a salary hike, then ask for it now. In all probability, this will be honoured. A woman will play an important role in your career now. She is headstrong and opinionated and cannot be trifled with. She could be your senior. You may have to work closely with her. There will be progress in your career as I see the difficult phase ebbing and good times on the horizon.

July

If you are looking for a job, then there is good news around the corner. An overseas opportunity may well be on its way to you. In an existing job, your work will pick up and you will be doing rather well. You may get into a partnership or a joint venture involving another person. If you have had a dream regarding a certain job, role, business or a concept, then it will materialize this July. You will manifest your heart's desire with this life-changing opportunity.

August

Success and satisfaction are well within your grasp. All you need to do now is to focus on your work. However, if something is troubling you, then this may be the time to introspect and look within for the answers you are seeking. Simply take a quiet walk or lock yourself in a room and meditate over the problem. A woman will be your ally this month. She will support you through your difficulties and help you out with work issues. The month will end with something troubling you. You may turn into your greatest adversary and take people's opinions and remarks way too personally. Do not act in the heat of the moment and don't let people and judgements get to you.

September

If you are expecting news of a job offer or role change, then it is likely to get delayed further. It will come eventually but you may have to wait a little longer for it. A man who is authoritative and experienced will mentor you through your existing projects or assignments. His influence is positive and under his able guidance you will learn well. The month will end beautifully and I see you reaping the fruits of your labour. You will achieve what you have been working on relentlessly.

October

If you are not happy in your current job, then now is the time to act. Don't remain in a job that does not satisfy you. However, if you are seeking a job, go slow. Do not act out of desperation and don't lose heart if there is a delay. Your job will come to you when you attract it through a positive state of mind. Mid-month, your work will pick up once again. You will have every reason to rejoice and make merry. There will be reunions, cultural events, parties, etc., where people will come together and make merry.

November

Work will pick up and you should be doing rather well now. After all, you have survived the stormy nights and internal conflicts and emerged victorious. But now may not be the time to slack off. Your work is being observed. If you are working diligently, the outcome will be good. But if success has gone to your head and you have become complacent, then you may just be hauled up for it. The month will end on a good note with your work moving in a positive direction. Accomplishments and success will be yours again.

December

If you are awaiting results which are dependent on other people's decisions, then you may have to wait longer than you thought.

Nevertheless, the final outcome is going to be positive and it will culminate in an opportunity. A man, who could be your senior in your work set-up, will be supportive of you. Your work will be going rather well towards the end of the year. You will have a great deal to be proud of and your co-workers will recognize your tireless efforts and reward you for them. You will receive these rewards in the form of a bonus, a salary increase or an incentive. Overall, 2018 will be good for your career.

CAPRICORN

THE DEVIL

Love Forecasts

January

The year will start off well and I see you comfortably placed in a relationship with your partner. If you are awaiting positive news or some development, then you will receive this soon. Unfortunately, as the month progresses, small issues, arguments and conflicts may crop up. You should know when to push your viewpoint and when to back off. If you are keen to take a break, I suggest you do so even if it is only for a few days to spend some time with yourself. This breather will help both you and your partner get much-needed clarity.

The single attractive Capricorn will meet someone very exciting and interesting this month. However, if you don't show interest in this suitor, then chances are that he/she may move on to someone else.

February

You may have to moderate various aspects to strike a balance in your love life. You could be juggling two important facets of your existence, such as your work and love life. This multitasking is going to be difficult but making time for love is as important as putting bread and butter on the table. There could be emotional issues and an upheaval in your relationship towards the end of the month. If you are having a conflict with your partner, don't jump to conclusions and do not take hasty decisions like ending the relationship.

The single Capricorn who is seeking love will see victory this month. You will be at the top of the game and you could be getting ready to commit to the one you so deeply desire.

March

There is an element of one-upmanship between you and your partner. You need to determine whether you are playing ego games with each other. Both of you are completely in love with each other and this could be one of the finest phases of your love life. In fact, if you made a wish in love, I am certain it would be granted. If you have the tendency to get impatient with your partner and expect immediate gratification, then you may have to alter this attitude. Slow down and be patient.

The unattached Capricorn will be hopelessly attracted to a woman beyond his reach. If you are a woman Capricorn, then people will be falling over themselves to proclaim their love interest in you.

April

You will be torn between love and another aspect of life, making balance impossible in life. Later in the month, your work will keep you too busy to give time to your relationship. If you continue to give so much attention to your career, your love life will suffer. The woman in this relationship will take complete control. She will chalk out a plan to restore the balance in this relationship and strengthen the love bond.

If you are seeking love, then this is the time to be patient. Desperation will only push your luck away. You must wait for the right time and the right suitor to come along.

May

This month, you may reach a phase in your relationship when you will be feeling bored and uninterested. You will notice that the chemistry is missing and find yourself questioning your partner's contribution to the relationship. The way I see it, you need to change your perspective to adapt to the changing times. Mid-month, I see that both of you will work together to strengthen your bond. There is balance when there is give and take by both partners.

The single Capricorn will spend too much time procrastinating and worrying about love. You must take it easy and wait for the right time to strike.

June

You will be doing rather well in your love relationship this month. But if you and your partner desire to take a break together or separately, June may be a good time for this. Don't cling to your partner if he/she decides to take a break alone. Mid-month, I see your relationship progressing well and you may decide to take it to the next level of commitment and consider marriage, an engagement or a live-in arrangement. But if you have any areas of concern in this relationship, then you must speak up and clarify these doubts with your partner.

The unattached Capricorn will be too busy with work to make time for love. This will lower your chances of finding the perfect suitor.

July

A woman will influence your love life this month. She could be your mother, sister or a friend. This influence will be negative so you should avoid getting influenced by this person. Mid-month, your relationship will witness a stable phase provided your partner treats you as an equal. If your partner isn't fair, then it may be time to speak up and take some important decisions. The end of the month may not be such a good time for your relationship. You have done everything in your capacity to save it but it may be beyond repair.

If you are unattached, this month will bring in some good news. You will soon meet someone exciting and intriguing who will turn out to be the perfect suitor.

August

August will be a beautiful month for your love relationship. Your partner will reciprocate your feelings and demonstrate just how much he/she loves you. It is wonderful to know that someone you care about returns your feelings. I see you involved in parties and anniversaries with your beloved where you will celebrate your love and share your joy with your family and friends.

The single Capricorn will go through a challenging phase this month. You may realize that the person you are interested in isn't thinking about you in the same way. This will leave you heartbroken.

September

A conflict is likely to take place this month which will shake the foundation of your relationship. It is best to approach the issue with an open mind and weigh your options. As the month progresses, your relationship will improve. You may realize that your partner loves you as much as you love him/her. This revelation will help you change your perspective and restore the peace and love in your relationship. The man in this relationship is headstrong, highly opinionated and tough to handle. If you are the female Capricorn, you will have to accept your male partner as he is and manage him gently.

The single Capricorn who is seeking love will receive good news this September. You will initiate a relationship with someone you dearly love.

October

If you have been facing issues in your relationship, then this may be a make-or-break time for it. Either the two of you will decide to stay together for good or you will part ways amicably. If you do manage to stay together, then this relationship will undergo a transformation with the announcement of marriage or news that you will be starting a family. If having a baby was never part of the plan, then it will make sense to take precautions now. You must learn to relinquish old hang-ups and issues that are causing problems and move on. Avoid being overprotective or too possessive at this juncture.

The unattached Capricorn will witness a transformational change this month. You may have to end an ongoing association to start a new one, which will begin with the promise of love and renewal.

November

November will be a fabulous time for your relationship. I see your bond growing stronger and reaching a stage of deep love and understanding. The woman partner has played an important role in establishing the foundation of this relationship and seeing it grow from there. The month will end with some good news.

If you are seeking love, then this month may not bring in such good news. In fact, you may realize that the person you had set your heart on doesn't feel the same way about you.

December

You could be on the verge of initiating a new journey in love, something you have not done before. This could mean marriage, an engagement or simply declaring your commitment to your partner. However, the year will not end all that well for you. An unexpected revelation will upset the harmony you have established in this relationship. You may decide to sever this bond of love on the basis of this disclosure.

The unattached Capricorn may have to change his/her perspective in order to attract true love. If you have been approaching love with traditional beliefs, then it is time you grew emancipated.

Health Forecasts

January

I see you making the necessary changes to your lifestyle at the start of this year. You may have to cut back on some indulgences, introduce exercise into your daily routine, eat right, sleep well and plan your life keeping your health in mind. Any health issues that emerge this month may be the result of repressed emotions which have gone unnoticed for too long. You could be at an all-time low both emotionally and physically and feeling lonely towards the end of the month. If this is the case, ask your near and dear ones for help.

February

Your health will be on an upswing at the start of this month. You will be involved in physical training and other forms of exercise. However, be careful and protect yourself from injury. If you are already injured, go slow and don't overdo any training routine that could worsen the situation. Your health and life will be in a state of complete imbalance in the last few days of the month. You should focus on moderation and do everything within limits. The more balanced you are in your approach towards life and yourself, the better it will be for both body and mind.

March

You will make slow and gradual progress towards recovering from your health issue. If you have been advised to slow down and take it easy, then you should do so. You may have to initiate a short-term partnership with a health practitioner or a healer of some sort who will help you achieve your health goal. But you will need to watch where you are headed in terms of your stress levels. Do remember to meditate regularly and keep your stress levels in check. At this point, there may be other factors of your life that may be causing you stress.

April

If you have been worrying about your health, then you should consider relaxing and changing your mindset. Be optimistic and positive if you are awaiting test results or health outcomes. The more you worry, the more your health will suffer. I see that your test results and any awaited outcomes will be good, which will cheer you up. The month will end well and a new healer or a doctor will help you with your ailment. He/she will be an answer to your prayers in health. I am sure his/her intervention will go a long way in solving your health issues.

May

You will be stressed this month because of problems at work and other aspects of your life. You will be worried and feeling defeated and tired, and will be ready to give up. Hang in there and you will witness success. A man will be part of your health scene this month. He will be someone who sets rules and protocols. You will need to make an important change or alteration in yourself this month. This will be related to your bad habits or vices. If you have the tendency to binge drink or are inclined towards substance abuse, then correct these habits right away. You must fight such temptations with a strong will.

June

I see you struggling between conflicting elements – your work and personal life, your health and work, etc. – and trying hard to establish common ground. You could be trying hard to figure out the cause of your health issues. Instead of searching for the answers, let them come to you. If you are still unable to find answers to your questions regarding your health, then perhaps you should consider the spiritual angle. For example, if you are suffering from chronic backache or leg pain, you could be carrying too much 'weight' metaphorically speaking.

July

You have reason to cheer up and make merry this month. The news you will receive will be positive and will allay all your health-related suspicions and doubts. You may be involved in happy events and functions and will be able to infect others with your positive emotions. But be careful about how you conduct yourself in your health routines and rituals. In all probability, you will be overdoing something. The times are about to change and the ostrich-with-its-head-in-the-sand attitude will not go down well for you in your current situation. You must steel yourself for what lies ahead and take it in your stride.

August

You will experience a heightened sense of emotional well-being. Feelings of happiness and stability will make your life complete. You have an excellent support system in the form of a loving family, and this is your greatest weapon in fighting any health ailment. A little further into the month and you will encounter a strong, determined man who is an authoritative figure. He may play an important role in your treatment as a healer, or may have an impact in other areas of your life. You will feel beaten, battered and defeated at some point and may decide to cut and run. Hang in there a little longer and you will witness success in the aspect of life where you felt defeated.

September

You may experience some upheavals in other areas of your life this month which will disturb the balance in your health. I see something ending for you. You will take the necessary action and move on in your life after this change which may not be easy to adapt to. It will bring its own set of worries and anxieties but the good news is that I see you dealing with it well. Mid-month, your health will be looking up and you will be happy and content with the way your life has panned out. Your test results and other aspects of your health will be normal and the news in general will be positive and happy. Someone will step forward to either financially aid your treatment, or proffer help in the form of healing.

October

You will be worried about your health this month but most of your pessimistic thoughts will be based on imaginary fears. Hence it is best that you focus on realigning yourself to optimism and being happy. Mid-month, you may find yourself euphoric when one of your greatest health wishes will come true. At this time, if you ask for anything, in all likelihood you will receive it. The month will end with certain changes coming your way, and the success of your health will depend on how you adapt to this new situation. It is also possible that your health may go through turbulence, but this will be something you can deal with.

November

You could witness some difficult situations which will upset you. This is the time when you must follow your intuition. If you have doubts about a treatment or diagnosis, then take a second opinion. Do everything you can to put your doubts to rest. If you have been indulging in substance abuse, then know where you are headed and consider the consequences of your actions. The month will end on a happy note with some good news coming your way. This news may be of childbirth or pregnancy.

December

You have the fortitude to physically and mentally overcome the odds you are facing. If your health has been poor, then know that you will be able to beat the ailment. Mid-month, there will be some revelations which may cause an emotional tumult. This truth will leave you shaken, and you will be unable to digest the facts that have emerged. But you must remember to stay strong. This is the time to take utmost care of your health, especially your emotional health. Worry, anxiety or depression will only exacerbate your problems. If you are facing these issues, then it is time you put your best foot forward and be brave.

Wealth Forecasts

January

The year has begun and you will also be making some interesting plans related to your finances. You will be seeking guidance from financial planners or advisers who will help you formulate a strong investment structure for your money. You are likely to follow the traditional approach to investing and use the standard protocols to maximize your gains. You could also consider sharing your abundance with the needy which will help you get more back.

February

You will be on the horns of a dilemma about which investment avenues will be most beneficial. Evaluating all the options and researching them thoroughly will help you make a good choice. Don't take a hasty decision which you will regret later. Your money situation is likely to improve to a great extent this month. You will receive news of a sudden influx of funds which you didn't expect. Your income from business will also be looking good at this time. In fact, if you are considering your own venture, this may be the right time to go ahead with it.

March

You will be worried about your financial situation this month because you have too many expenses and too little income. Mid-month, you will make a major purchase such as a car or tickets for a vacation. This is great considering that you were in a tight financial position a little earlier in the month. But do not go overboard with your spending, and pause for a minute to consider if this expenditure is really necessary. Prioritize your spending and use this resource for important financial obligations first.

April

The two elements – your income and your expenses – will be out of kilter with no parity between what comes in and what goes out. You might have to pay close attention to the way you are managing your finances. Mid-month, you may shut down a source of revenue which will make your financial situation tight. But the decision to bring this revenue stream to an end was imperative since it failed to give results.

May

You may receive a windfall which will set the course for wealth to flow freely towards you. But this doesn't mean that you should splurge. You may be involved in a game of chance later this month. I see you getting lucky in ways you didn't expect. To make your luck last, you need to have faith in yourself. Mind the gap between what you want to achieve and what you believe you can achieve. If you think that your bad luck will overrule all the good you have done, then this is probably what will happen. Hence it is about time you broke loose from such pessimism.

June

Your financial situation will change and money will make its way to you. If you are employed, then expect a sudden bonus or a raise. If you are in business, then your profits will surge. Money will come to you in one way or the other. You will also receive financial investments when you least expect them this month. Don't squander all this wealth. Put it to good use and ensure your money works for you and makes you more.

July

You may receive money from work, investments, a lottery or even an inheritance this month. You need to focus on using this wealth prudently and for a good purpose. It is quite possible that you may not be able to meet all your financial obligations this month. But this is only a temporary situation, until the money comes in. The end of the month is the time to take precautions. If you are planning to invest money, then do so conservatively and in risk-free avenues. Avoid taking major financial decisions or making investments this month, and watch where you are putting your money.

August

You will reap the rewards for all your efforts and good deeds – something that you gave out which the universe has returned to you with interest. The rewards will come in the form of money. You deserve every bit of this influx and should make the most of it. If you have been thinking about starting a business, now may be the time to go ahead and fulfil this desire. However, back up your ideas and desires with thorough research and study the potential of these ideas to know their viability. The end of the month will be the time to apply moderation to the way you spend your money.

September

You may be struggling with your income and expenses. What you need to remember is that you have the ability to turn your financial situation around. The best way to do this is to believe in yourself, think positively and harness your inner strength. Towards the end of the month, you will take control of your situation and devise ways and means to turn it all around. A woman may help you in planning and achieving your financial goals. She is intelligent and an expert in finance.

October

Money will be scarce and there will be too many expenses to deal with. But what happens next will surprise you. You will witness a sudden turn of events and money will flow to you in an unimaginable way. You may suddenly receive a bonus or an incentive, returns on your investments, or your business profits may go through the roof. The month will end in a manner that is the opposite of the way it started. You will be in a good position financially and a family inheritance or even money from gambling or a lottery may unexpectedly come to you and completely bowl you over.

November

You will be getting ready to invest in home renovations to add more comfort and luxury to your surroundings. However, taking up a big mortgage or a large loan will spoil the fun. I see some imbalance once again in your money management. This could be because you may be investing too much in the home renovations. The month will end with your money situation improving. You could be getting ready for a big ticket purchase like a house.

December

A woman will play an important role in shaping your finances this month. She is good at financial planning and her expert advice will help you manage your wealth in a better way. If you are worried about your money, then work towards fixing the problems instead of procrastinating. Surprisingly, the year will end on a good note. If the flow of money to you was blocked, then this will change now. Once again apply caution to the way you spend your money and use it in the best possible way. Before I end this chapter, I would like to give you some friendly advice. In your wealth predictions, I have often noticed an imbalance and the tendency to splurge. This indicates that you are unleashing the indulgent side of your personality more than needed. It will be in your best interest to keep this aspect of your personality in check.

Career Forecasts

January

You will be anticipating a reward, increment or a promotion for all the good work you have done in the past. You know the reward will come, but it is taking too long. Needless to say, stay calm. You are likely to receive your reward in the second half of the month. It will come in the form of money or appreciation and accolades. However, towards the end of the month, you may face some conflict and you may feel the need to move on, but the comfort of a steady income and job security will hold you back.

February

Your conservative approach needs to be replaced by a new way of accomplishing tasks. If you want to settle down in your current role, then this change is mandatory. You can't continue to work in an old-fashioned way as that may hinder your progress. If you are looking for a job, then you need to project yourself as someone who is dependable. I see you getting into trouble mid-month when your work will be under scrutiny. This is the time to prove yourself. Defend your position by working in the manner expected of you and achieve the goals assigned to you. The work pressure will be overwhelming, and you are likely to take on more than you can handle.

March

If you have been waiting for a job offer or any other news related to your career, you can be assured that it will come soon. This will be an exciting new opportunity that will give you a new profile. Channelize your energy in achieving the tasks assigned and develop new and innovative ideas which will help you grow in your career. A connection from your past will emerge this month. You may come across someone who will help you connect the dots and achieve something thrilling in your career.

April

You have made up your mind to change jobs this month to follow your heart. In case you decide to stay where you are, you will find the tide shifting and your work situation will move into a positive zone. Money, appreciation and rewards will come in one way or the other. If you have been thinking about starting a business or doing something of your own, then now may be the time to do this. An influential man will be part of your work scene this month. He could be your boss or a senior who is difficult to deal with and not easy to impress. You may have trouble working closely with him, but if you are sincere and diligent, you will be able to establish a cordial work relationship with him.

May

You may have issues with people making personal remarks about you and putting you down this month. This will lead to heated arguments. Try to keep your cool as far as possible, and manage the situation without hurting or snubbing others. There is a very high possibility that you will feel betrayed and let down. Stay away from office politics and lie low. Beyond this phase lie rewards and success. You have worked very hard to get this far and I see you reaping the rewards for your efforts. People in general will be looking up to you and appreciating you as a role model. A young man could come along and offer you help in a way that could ease a lot of your work-related stress.

June

Someone may come along and offer you much-needed help in the form of a work-related opportunity or a financial raise that will reduce your worries. This will be in return for all your good karmic deeds in the past. You may undertake a lot of work-related travel. This is good news as it will expose you to different situations and give you some time off from your hectic work schedule.

If you are awaiting some news or looking for a job, then the news is likely to be good. You may find what you are seeking. You will be involved with some legal contracts and agreements and sign a new deal or an agreement which will be just and fair for your career prospects and your professional growth. Towards the end of the month, take care of your work–life balance.

July

You may undertake international travel through work which will add to your overall experience and sense of satisfaction. You may encounter feelings of defeat and feel disregarded by seniors or peers at work. This may lead you to show resentment towards your work and the people around you. This could make you your own worst enemy. You must stay calm, avoid picking fights and let this phase settle down. The month will end with some competition headed your way. If you are seeking a job, assignment or a certain client, then know this is not going to be easy since there is stiff rivalry with plenty of aspirants vying for this opportunity.

August

August brings good news mostly related to a promotion, salary hike or bonus, coming your way. You will be backed by an authoritative figure who will support you in your career this month. He could be a senior or an immediate boss who is kind and trustworthy. You can trust him completely and follow his lead. You must use his support and achieve the goals that have been chalked out for you. Use your creative abilities to innovate and devise new concepts and ideas.

September

If you are looking for a job, a good offer will come through in September. You may also move forward on a project that seemed stuck. You will have what you need to feel accomplished and successful this month. But if you are not satisfied with your existing work and have been feeling unhappy in your workplace, then it's time that you moved out and did something you truly enjoyed.

Mid-month, a change will be coming your way which will create an upheaval in your life and you may end up being pushed out of your job. Your work will seem very hectic towards the end of the month when there will be too much to do and you will not have enough energy to do it. Consider sharing your work burden with others so that you don't get overwhelmed, and are more productive.

October

You may start a new vocation or undertake a new job or a course that will enhance your performance in your career this month. Although it will be challenging, the rewards are guaranteed. In an existing job scenario, you could be feeling stuck but you may be unwilling to get out because of job security or financial reasons. Instead of brooding, you should take action to fulfil your wish in your career and move out of this thankless job. If you decide to stay on, then let this be your decision and take full responsibility for it. The month will end with a mentor, who could be a senior in your work set-up, entering your work scene.

November

It is quite possible that you are being paid too little for the amount of work you do. If this is the case, then now is the time to blow your own trumpet and proclaim your worth to those around you. Chances are that your demands will be heard. If your career decision depends on others, then know that it may take a while longer to materialize. However, if you have done your homework, then the decision is likely to be positive. Do not push people to take quick decisions, and act according to your position in your work set-up. This is also the time when you should consider changing your old ways of working. A traditional approach will impede your progress.

December

You may be bitterly caught up between your professional life and personal life. You must handle both well and establish a good work–life rapport before one or the other begins to suffer. Legal agreements and contracts could be headed your way this month. If you are feeling bored and trapped in your job, this will be because of your approach to it. You need to look at all the positives of your job before you point fingers at anyone. The year will end with harsh decisions. You may decide to leave your existing job as it has failed to meet your expectations. However, I am sure that something good will come out of this decision.

AQUARIUS

THE STAR

Love Forecasts

January

I see you getting ready to go on a short holiday at the start of the year. This may be with your partner or on your own. If your partner is keen to take a break alone, then happily allow him/her to do so. This is no time to make a scene by being clingy or needy. A break is always useful. You should count your blessings and thank the universe for the abundance it has bestowed on you. You have the perfect relationship. Towards the end of the month, you may experience a slight disconnect with your partner and your love life may lose its lustre. You may begin to take this relationship for granted, which is natural. But before you blame your partner, look within and question your contribution.

The single Aquarius will take some time off for a much-needed break this month. You will be able to think about love and explore all the possibilities available to you during this break. If you have recently separated from your partner, then this break will help you rejuvenate and heal.

February

You need to communicate directly and clearly with your partner this month and ensure there isn't any ambiguity or miscommunication. If anything is bothering you, discuss it with your partner. I see your relationship being renegotiated at this time. Whatever you have been doing until now may not suit the present situation. The month will end with you juggling your work and love life, both of which will be demanding.

If you are a single Aquarius seeking love, then don't get impatient and restless. Love will come if you believe in it and take the required action. Any desperate moves will only defeat the purpose.

March

If you are feeling restless and impatient about your love life, then calm down. You will receive a positive outcome if you are willing to be patient. You have done your bit and your partner will respond in time. Towards the middle of the month, you may decide to end the relationship or simply be detached from it. You will realize that there is little left for you in this relationship.

The unattached Aquarius will mostly get over a recent break-up but may still not be emotionally ready to commit to a new relationship. Hence, it is important to get out and put yourself in a space where you can find love instead of brooding over the past.

April

There may be a lot of conflict and arguments in your relationship this month. Be prepared to hold your ground and deal with differences of opinion gently and graciously. You may discover that your partner doesn't reciprocate your love which will leave you feeling devastated. Towards the end of the month, emotional upheaval and stress will resurface and disturb the harmony in your relationship. You could be involved in heated arguments, fights and drama which will drain you. Stay strong and you will discover that this cloud has a silver lining.

There will be good news for the single Aquarius seeking love. You will meet someone exciting and intriguing this month. This person is young and bright and will add a spark to your love life.

May

You will witness a positive phase of recovery when the situation will improve and your problems will settle down. You or your partner, whoever is the man in the relationship, is headstrong and highly opinionated. This may become a problem for your relationship but you can't do much about it. If you are the female partner in this relationship, you would be advised to adopt a gentle approach with your tough lover. The month will end with some good news. If you have been planning to get married or have a baby, then this is likely to happen this month.

The single Aquarius will experience some mental stress this month due to other aspects of life. You will need to deal with these issues first before you can attract the right suitor.

June

You could be eagerly awaiting a commitment from your partner and you may even push him/her to expedite it. This approach won't help. However, the best way to achieve a result will be to act aloof towards him/her and you could turn the situation around. Stay positive and you will see the tide turn in your favour. The end of the month will be a time for moderation and synergy between your ideas and those of your partner.

The unattached Aquarius will be getting ready to get into a relationship with a person he/she most desires. This is great and I wish you my best.

July

Your love life will be on an upswing this month with the person you love reciprocating your feelings. Knowing how much you are loved will only add to the happiness and peace in this relationship. You will be busy spending time with your partner and doing everything, including buying expensive gifts, to please him/her. You may decide to go on a short holiday, probably overseas, which will give you an opportunity to spend time with each other and build a strong foundation of love. News of childbirth may come along in mid-July.

If you are seeking love, then an opposite who is much older than you will enter your love scene this month. You will be attracted to him, but do not rule him out because of his age.

August

You could go through a phase of stagnation and boredom in your love life this month. If you have been feeling disconnected, it is time you worked on your relationship. Before you begin pointing fingers, correct your own mistakes. A need for change may arise in the middle of the month; both of you will have to sit down at this time and work things out before it is too late. This may mean renegotiating the terms of your relationship and finding solutions to your problems. The end of the month will not be such a good time for both of you, as I see suspicion and insecurity making matters worse. Both partners will not be entirely honest with each other.

The single Aquarius will feel beaten and battered with his/her career. I don't see you with any time left to find love or even to go looking for it. Try to achieve a work–life balance first.

September

I see you developing strategies and plans to improve your love life. You will move into a comfortable space with your partner at the end of the month when you will enjoy love and harmony. Your love life can't get better than this.

If you are unattached, you may be competing for your love interest's attention or you will have many suitors vying for your attention.

October

You will be ready to work on your relationship and explore new avenues to rekindle the spark. This initiative is great and I am sure your partner will notice and appreciate your efforts. You will be excited and eager to act on your ideas. But before you initiate these ideas, take a close look to understand if you are fulfilling your duties and responsibilities in this relationship. If not, then you may need to act on this first before tackling other issues. The end of the month will be a good time for your relationship when I see your partner reciprocating your feelings of love.

If you are unattached and looking for love, then you will first need to correct the imbalance in your life. You could be caught between two potential partners and dealing with them both at the same time. This could get difficult; hence it is imperative that you make a choice.

November

You and your partner will face some tough times this month and your interaction will be marked by conflict, heated arguments and emotional turmoil. Most of these worries emerge from insecurity and are only a figment of your imagination. It is important that you stay positive and avoid pessimism about the future of your relationship. You will see happiness towards the end of the month and manifest your greatest desire in love. If you have set your heart on a commitment, marriage, engagement or anything related to love, know that it will occur.

If you are a single Aquarius, you will get what you are seeking. If you have been losing hope about love, then know that all this will change and you will find true love soon.

December

You will find it difficult to give time and energy to your beloved. To solve this problem, you will have to make time for love in your hectic schedule. You should also consider a change in your attitude and perspective. You should understand that even a small change in the way you think can go a long way in fixing your issues related to love. The sooner you change your approach the better it will be for you.

The unattached Aquarius will have to moderate his/her hectic schedule to fit love in. You will have to look at the different aspects of your life and explore various possibilities to create time for love.

Health Forecasts

January

What you think is what you become. Positive thoughts will benefit your health. Since this is the first month of the year and a time for resolutions, I see you setting down some important goals such as being optimistic and avoiding negativity. Your eagerness to achieve these goals may lead you to a new partnership with a healer, doctor, fitness instructor or someone similar. Towards the end of the month, your health will be exceptionally good. If you are expecting test results and reports, then you are likely to get some good news.

February

There is perfect balance and harmony in your health this February. You will be eating right, sleeping well and exercising correctly, which together will produce positive results. Your body and mind will be in balance and you will do well spiritually too. A woman who is gentle and kind may be part of your health scene this month. Altruism will help you see problems in a different light and could also lead to solutions. You will face stiff competition towards the end of this month. You could be getting ready to participate in a marathon or some type of athletic event where victory will depend entirely on your performance.

March

You will receive good news this month if you are patient. It could be something that you are eagerly awaiting and related to test results and reports. Avoid getting stressed while you are waiting for the outcome. I see that a wish or a dream related to a certain level of fitness or health will be fulfilled. This news will lift your spirits. You will end the month feeling positive about your health.

April

You may be combating serious health issues which will get worse this April. I see you in a terrible state and feeling helpless and lonely. But this is only a phase and if you stay strong and positive, you will recover. You could be repressing your emotions which may be causing your health issues. I see that you have made up your mind to face the issues that have been holding you down and steeled yourself to take on this challenge this month. This is a good approach. What is important now is to channelize your energies and move ahead.

May

Your health will look good and you will begin to feel alive and fit again. This has happened due to your inner strength and your determination to fight the odds. I see you initiating something new like a fitness class, course or routine. This is going to be a challenge but discipline, persistence and hard work will go a long way in helping you achieve your health goals. Your willingness to work hard is what matters. But do not trust people so easily. Someone may cheat you or lie to your face. This could be your health practitioner or some other people in your life. If doubts arise, get a second opinion.

June

You could face a situation when your inner voice tells you one thing and the people around you tell you something else. In such a situation, you should simply follow your intuition which is your best guide. I see you happy and healthy in the middle of the month which will be a good time for your health. You may decide to take a short break, maybe an international trip, which will keep you fit, and refresh you. I see that childbirth may take place at this time. You may arrive at a stage when some harsh truths will surface and run you down. Your health will decline and you may begin to lose hope. Try to deal with the situation calmly.

July

You must review your daily routine and ensure that you eat right, sleep tight and exercise regularly. Meditate once in a while and take time off to relax and spend some time with yourself. If you get serious about your daily habits, your health issues will begin to recede. Let go of your past emotional baggage such as anger, hatred or feelings of guilt. Learn to forgive and forget. You will start something new mid-month. This may mean a new treatment or a routine which is different and somewhat challenging. Nevertheless, I want to remind you that you have what it takes to accomplish any task.

August

A very strong man will enter your health scene this month. He is determined and knowledgeable and could be a professional health practitioner or an instructor. If you doubt this health practitioner's opinions or are not entirely convinced about his diagnosis, do a thorough research and take a second opinion if required. You should clear all your doubts before you begin any medical intervention. The end of the month will be a good time for your health and I see you feeling energetic and recharged. Your efforts will begin to pay off and you will be at your fittest.

September

I see you struggling to keep up with your health regimen because other aspects of your life, such as your work, family, etc., will compete for your time. Set your priorities and focus on your health. Do not let other aspects of your life come in your way. Your work will take its toll on your health this month and I see you juggling various elements to strike a balance. It is good that you are using this time to prioritize your health. Continue to make time for your health while also doing what is required for your work, and you will get some respite soon.

October

Your stress levels will shoot up this month and this will interfere with your health. Your mind will play antics and fuel your stress and worry. But worrying is not the solution to your problem; instead relax and meditate. The middle of the month will be unimaginably good for you and you will attract the right partner who will help you heal. This partnership will be with a doctor, healer or an instructor who can make a real difference to your health.

November

This month, you will take on a new initiative in the form of a partnership or an association with someone who can make a difference to your health. Besides this initiative, you will have to deal with past emotional baggage which will be of prime importance this month. The month will end well and I see you recovering from your ailment. However, if you have sustained injuries in the process of recovery, try to slow down so that you don't create more pain or hurt yourself again. Be conservative in your approach and remain calm and centred.

December

You will need to let go of old wounds from the past and look at life with a new perspective. I see you embarking on a new initiative in health in the middle of the month. You may take up a new programme or course or start something which you feel strongly about. This is a perfect way to end the year. Nevertheless, success in this plan or initiative entails sacrifices. This may mean changing your attitude to life in general and making drastic lifestyle changes. Doing this is not going to be easy but if you do succeed, then the rewards will be huge.

Wealth Forecasts

January

The year will start well for you and you will have sufficient to take care of your own expenses and those of your family. You may also consider sharing your abundance with the less fortunate. Your finances will see growth this month and you will receive good returns on your investments. You will receive positive news mid-month which will cheer you up. Towards the end of the month, you will decide to renovate or refurbish your home or office space to add luxury and comfort to it. But while doing so, ensure that you don't take on more debt than you can comfortably repay.

February

Your financial situation is highly dependent on the way you think – whether you have positive or negative thoughts. So choose to be optimistic. As the month progresses, I see you trying very hard to innovate and create new ideas and opportunities which can generate wealth. In all probability, you will devise a brilliant concept which will help you achieve your financial goals, but you will need to act fast. The month will end with some stress and you will be worried about meeting your expenses. If you run a business, now may be the time to set up for collection or recovery activities. If your financial decisions depend on someone else, take action before it's too late.

March

Your finances will be at an all-time low this month. This is because your cash flow may be disrupted and your income from investments may also have declined. All you can do is to accept the reality of the situation and be patient until this phase blows over and the situation improves. You may have to make a sacrifice or a compromise, such as accepting a job or signing a contract which will generate far less income than what you are used to. But this is a good start, and this small compromise will lead to big rewards. The month will end with a small financial dilemma where a choice may fluster you.

April

You will receive some good news or, rather, you will receive an unexpected windfall this month which will help you recover from the deficits you faced last month. If you are involved in a business, then your profits will be on an upswing. If you have been considering starting a business of your own, this may be a good time to do so. You may take up a partnership or a venture with another person. The month will end with some good news coming your way. This will be related to a job offer or something similar which you have been expecting and which will set the course for a new beginning.

May

In the first half of the month, you may have to end an ongoing arrangement or a set-up which no longer yields the desired results. This will be a disheartening and difficult decision, but it is imperative that you end this arrangement and stop wasting your time, effort and money on it. You can put your resources to better use somewhere else, where the returns are more promising.

A man who is authoritative and knowledgeable will come along and help you sort out your finances. His ideas and thoughts will help you to a great extent. As you move closer to the end of the month, I see your financial situation improving and you will have enough to spend and save.

June

Although there will be cash inflows from varied sources such as an inheritance, lottery and gambling, the money will be accompanied by fears and insecurities. I see you troubled with money issues which may simply be a figment of your imagination. The more you worry the more your money will slip away from you. Hence it is best to relax. Your greatest financial wish or dream will be fulfilled in the second half of the month. This could be the ideal job, project, business account or a timely return on investments which will take care of all your expenses and allay your financial insecurities.

July

Your tight financial situation will change if you are willing to make a small sacrifice or a compromise this month. This will turn the wheel of fortune in your favour. You should consider sharing your wealth or whatever little you have with someone who is in need. As you move further into the month, you will be prompted to take an important decision about choosing a financial avenue or an investment opportunity. The month will end with some good news. You will receive a substantial sum of money for all your hard work.

August

You will initiate a partnership or a joint venture that promises substantial returns. This venture will be short-lived and should prove lucrative. A little further into the month, you will hear some positive news. You will see opportunities open up and money will start to flow in again. You should go slow with spends and put your money to good use. If you feel you have extra money, share it with someone who needs it.

September

You will be compelled to conclude an arrangement which has failed to deliver the promised results. But if it has been failing to perform, won't it make more sense to withdraw from it and save what you can in terms of money, time and effort? The decision to terminate this arrangement will be difficult but imperative. It may lead you to discover a hidden talent in yourself.

As you explore further, you will realize that this talent has the potential to generate wealth in a way that you never thought about before. Your finances will only get better as the month progresses. You will discover that you have surplus wealth and can fulfil all your material needs.

October

If you were facing any kind of blockage in your wealth generation, then you will find that this no longer exists and money will flow in again. Be prudent and set aside something for a rainy day. Your money situation may not always remain as it is now. In fact, as the month progresses, your financial situation may get tight. In such a scenario, you should remain positive, accept the reality of the situation and, if your heart so desires, share whatever you can with the less fortunate.

November

Your financial position may get difficult this month and you may have to spend more than you earn to meet your expenses. This may cause you stress and tension. Tarot indicates a time of hope and positive reinforcements. You must know that your financial dream or goal will become a reality if you are willing to wait it out and be patient. If you give up now, all your efforts which have brought you so far will become futile. You will face more difficulties towards the end of the month when a revelation will bring your dream castle crumbling down. Although the situation may seem challenging, it will eventually change, as change is the only constant.

December

You will have to choose between various options which will put you in a dilemma. Go slow, back up your decision with sound research and you will be able to proceed in the right direction. In the second half of the month, you will be exceptionally busy renovating your home or office to add luxury and comfort to these spaces. This is a good decision provided you stay within your limits. This concludes your wealth predictions for 2018. Let's move onto your career readings.

Career Forecasts

January

A person senior in both age and authority will come to your aid in January. He will either offer an opportunity which is life-changing or give you financial aid which will help you considerably. This benevolence is repayment for your good deeds in the past. However, a little further into the month, I see trouble brewing for you. You may become your own enemy, beset by pessimism about your work and the people around you. This negativity could emerge from a defeat or because of your seniors and peers disregarding your work. You will receive positive outcomes towards the end of month which will cheer you up and give you the faith to move on.

February

Beware of treachery, deceit and distrust which will occur this month. Someone may not be entirely honest with you and could stab you in the back. Do not trust people easily and watch out for the games people play. Mid-month, you may decide to take a break or consider a change. This break may be short but it will do you good and give you some much-needed clarity. You may decide to quit your present work set-up and take a few days off before you start something new and challenging. You may face imbalance and chaos in your career at this stage. If you do everything in moderation, you will be able to accomplish all your tasks, and these accomplishments will be noticed.

March

You will become lackadaisical in your work and lose the passion that you once had for it. You need to find a way to recharge and regain your motivation to work. In my opinion, you are blaming external factors for your apathy instead of looking deep within yourself. Mid-month, you may decide to follow your heart and move on to do something which is challenging and exciting. This is an excellent decision and I see that you will be able to achieve what you desire. Towards the end of the month, you will take on a new responsibility in the form of a partnership or a venture involving another person.

April

You have toiled hard and now is the time to enjoy the fruits of your labour. Accolades and appreciation will be showered upon you. However, as the month progresses, I see you terminating your association with something that has failed to deliver results despite all your efforts. This could be a business unit, an assignment, project or a job. This association may be at an end but a new beginning awaits you. You will take the decision to move on and end what you have given your best to with a heavy heart. A woman will be your ally and help you through this month.

May

Your work will be on an upswing at the start of this month. I see you undertaking a lot of travel, meeting new people and expanding your network. Unfortunately, the situation could get heated at your workplace as your seniors and peers will make certain comments or pass judgements that may seem unfair. You could be reading too much into the situation. Learn to stay calm, do not get into heated arguments with colleagues and definitely avoid jumping to conclusions or taking hasty decisions. The month will end beautifully. You will emerge victorious, unshaken and unscathed. What doesn't kill you makes you stronger.

June

Your work will be under scrutiny this month; so you need to focus and put in extra effort. If you have been working well, the rewards are guaranteed, but if you have been lax, then now is the time to get your act together. Mid-month, you could find yourself stuck between a rock and a hard place. If this is the case, then a balance is needed. The month will end with uncertainty and emotional upheaval. You will be trapped in a situation where everything seems to be going against you and you may wonder whether you truly deserve this. Well honestly, if you just give it some time and calmly deal with what comes your way, you will emerge victorious from this situation.

July

You will be aware that someone is working against you but reacting to this person will not be the solution. Don't let small issues get blown out of proportion; instead handle the situation with calm and poise. As the month progresses, you will find that this problem affecting you more than it should. You could feel trapped in a job that you detest, but due to the security of a regular pay cheque and job stability you are unable to move on. Towards the end of the month, you may receive some good news.

August

You could receive some disturbing news about a colleague playing politics, leaving you feeling distraught. Mid-month, you could be getting ready to bring about a positive change in your attitude which will reduce the involvement of your ego and enable you to accept what comes your way more pragmatically. The other interpretation of this change is that you may have to make a compromise or a sacrifice in terms of your position, job or a reduction in salary to adapt to what comes next. Although adapting to the change won't be easy, it is mandatory. The good news is that the outcome of this small change is going to be highly rewarding, hence it makes sense for you to accept what comes your way gracefully. You could initiate a new partnership towards the end of the month.

September

If you are looking for a job, then a good offer is winging its way to you. If you are happy with your existing job, you will find that your work is appreciated and your colleagues will turn to you for your valuable advice. A woman who is authoritative and senior in age will mentor you. The month will end with a man influencing your career. This person may be the top boss or a person with the highest authority. He is kind and likes you. He will support you in your work and facilitate your growth and progress.

October

This month, you will create a new idea, procedure or protocol that will ease everyone's life. Accomplishing this is not going to be easy but you will beat the odds and achieve the impossible. This is the time when new ideas and thoughts will flow in and, if acted upon, can make a big difference in your life. However, look out for the unrealistic work pressure that comes along mid-month. You will be overwhelmed and stressed with all the work you have taken on. A man will enter your work scene at the end of the month.

November

You may be asked to leave your job, or there may be some other development of great magnitude, which will shatter your dreams and cause you considerable stress. Otherwise too, the situation at work may get heated with frequent arguments and conflicts. You will have to stay strong through this period and remain focused on your career goals. The forthcoming days will be more positive and I see your work looking very good by the middle of the month. You may become indispensable at your workplace. But do not get carried away with your success. Reaching the top is easy but staying there can be a challenge.

December

You could move on from your job to pursue a hobby or a passion, or simply because the present arrangement didn't work out for you. This is the best decision considering your options now. I see new contracts and agreements coming your way. With time, you will begin to reap the rewards for all your efforts. These rewards will come in the form of money or better opportunities. All that you need to do is believe in yourself and be patient. You have come a long way and done exceptionally well in your career this year. I pray you stay focused and continue to do your best in the year to come.

PISCES

THE MOON

Love Forecasts

January

You may become possessive this month and cling more than necessary to your partner. Remember this may suffocate your partner and drive him/her away. You will receive some disheartening news later in the month. You may realize this relationship was never meant to be and the person you so dearly love doesn't feel the same way about you.

If you are a single Pisces seeking love, then let go of the image you have of the perfect lover or the ideal relationship. The longer you hold on to these notions, the further you will push your luck away.

February

You will have everything that you want in your love life – stability, love, respect, a harmonious relationship and a perfect lover. You couldn't ask for more. I see you travelling and exploring places with your beloved. By the end of the month, you will reap the rewards for all your efforts in this relationship. Your partner will value your efforts and reciprocate accordingly. This is a beautiful and magical time for your relationship. Make the most of it.

The unattached Pisces will be goal-oriented and determined to make love happen this month. But if someone is pushing you into a relationship, you will need to decide if this is something that you really want.

March

You will decide to take your love to the next level this month. You may consider proposing and expressing your love to your beloved in the most romantic way possible. Towards the end of the month, a man who is senior to you could influence your relationship. You will need to balance your life and get more organized in the way you conduct yourself in love at this time. If you have been losing your focus in love, it's time you gave this aspect of your life the priority it deserves.

The Pisces who is seeking love will find answers in his/her past. Something or someone from the past may emerge and open an avenue to opportunities in love. For all you know your former lover may reappear in your life and your old feelings could be rekindled.

April

You will initiate a new beginning in matters of the heart. This may mean marriage, a live-in arrangement or an official declaration of love. As the month progresses, your relationship will get even stronger. A woman who is hot-headed, opinionated and interfering could play a crucial role in your love life this month. You must keep her intervention to the minimum so as to safeguard your love interest. This woman could be your mother, sister or a friend.

The unattached Pisces may be recuperating from a failed relationship. This will make it difficult for you to focus on opportunities in love. But if you have to move on, then the sooner you recover from this break-up, the better it will be.

May

You are driven and committed to make this relationship last, and you are ready to do whatever it takes in this regard. All your efforts will pay off and you and your lover will share a strong bond of love. Your relationship will be based on maturity and understanding. However, towards the end of the month, it would be wise for you to give your partner some space. This is not the time to cling to each other or act desperate.

The unattached Pisces will see some positive outcomes in love this month. You may meet someone exciting through your work. Keep your eyes and ears open for this possibility.

June

You will have everything you need to feel secure and loved. As the month progresses, you will be even more emotionally inclined to your partner and he/she will reciprocate your feelings. There is romance and a strong chemistry between the two of you. You will be planning an event together which will give you a reason to cheer. This could be a birthday party, an anniversary celebration or a reunion.

If you are single, then get ready to be swept off your feet by someone charming and intensely attractive. You will be head over heels in love with this person.

July

If you feel trapped in a relationship in which you are feeling constrained because you don't have freedom of expression and can't be yourself, then it's better to communicate your feelings to your partner. You could be torn between different elements which may be difficult to synergize. This will cause an imbalance and make it difficult for you to focus on your love life. The best way to correct this imbalance is through moderation and tempering. Towards the end of the month, I see you taking drastic measures to rectify the errors that you committed earlier so that you can salvage your love relationship.

If you are single and seeking love, then it's about time you made love your focus, instead of work.

August

You will have everything you ever desired and you will be grateful to the divine for your beautiful gift of love. You will become inseparable in body, mind and spirit. You will experience an awakening, and this feeling of intense peace and happiness will only strengthen your individual perspectives as well as what you have together. Your relationship will simply keep growing and reach greater heights of happiness and joy.

The single Pisces will realize his/her dream in love and if you have been seeking a commitment, then it will fall into place this month.

September

You can't be happier than you are in your present relationship. You and your partner share a strong bond of hope, love and understanding. You could hear some good news and be emotionally uplifted this September. This news may be related to marriage which is in your cards. Your partnership has obviously reached a certain stage of stability and security for marriage to be initiated. You have my blessings for this wonderful climax to your relationship.

The unattached Pisces will be getting ready to commit to his/her partner, but this person may not be ready for a serious step like this. Instead of pushing your choices on your partner, act distracted and you will succeed in capturing his/her attention.

October

This month, you and your partner will enjoy a stable relationship in which there is mutual give and take. You will share your responsibilities in a harmonious way which will strengthen your bond of love. If your partner offers financial aid and if you need it, you should go ahead and accept it. Later in the month, you may feel defeated and disregarded because arguments and conflicts may arise between you and your partner. In my opinion, you are taking these differences of opinion too far, and you should bring a stop to this conflict before it turns ugly.

If you are seeking love, then you should focus on your love prospects instead of trying to create more wealth. Don't focus on something else if you want a stable love life.

November

Balancing love and work is going to take its toll on you, but it is imperative that you establish a balance between these two elements. A little further in the month, serious issues will rock the foundation of your love life. Your relationship may be about to end or may have reached a stage when some sort of damage control is required to salvage it. If there is something troubling you about your relationship, or if you suspect there is something unhealthy in the background, acknowledge it and speak up right away instead of worrying about it.

The unattached Pisces will be getting ready to meet someone exciting and interesting this month. This meeting is likely to occur at a marriage function or some other event of this kind.

December

You may have reached a point of no return with your partner and are ready to separate by mutual consent. Although you will be pained and hurt by this decision, it is inevitable. In the unlikely event that you don't separate, you will experience a major imbalance in your relationship. You and your partner will not be in harmony with each other and you won't have peace of mind. A woman may be responsible for the problems in this relationship. This person could be a mother, sister or friend. I see you ending the year on a very painful note. You will be distraught because of the constant conflict in your relationship. At this stage, it is important to avoid heated discussions and hasty decisions.

The single Pisces will enjoy a positive phase at the end of the year. If you were hoping that a relationship would materialize, your wish is likely to be fulfilled with some important and incredible developments taking place in matters of the heart.

Health Forecasts

January

You will start the year feeling some amount of stress related to a dilemma you are in. You have to choose from various options and understand which choice suits your current situation. This decision could be related to a treatment option, health practitioners or something else related to your health. You may decide to take a break to simply relax and recuperate, or you may be hospitalized for a health condition. If it is hospitalization, it may be for a routine check-up or something minor that you can easily deal with. You will end the month with feelings of rejection, sadness and disappointment. You will be hurt with the way a certain situation has turned out.

February

You will have to fight the condition you are facing and I see you steeling yourself to take on what lies ahead. There could be some positive news or development which will motivate you to focus on your health optimistically. Watch the way you conduct your body and mind and strike a balance with respect to your work and health. I see you struggling to deal with some news you may have received or something that is likely to occur.

March

An obstacle you faced will be removed and I see you surging ahead in health matters. You will be emotionally stable and content with a general sense of well-being. Mid-month, I see you receiving rewards for your efforts. You will achieve your fitness goal, recover from your ailments and be successful with other health goals that you may have been working on. If you have been expecting a test result or a report and have been anticipating a negative outcome, change your thoughts and think positively. Stay calm and know that all will be well eventually.

April

You may be getting very restless waiting for some news or test results related to your health. Pessimism is not going to help. There is some regret or feelings of anger and hurt which were holding you back in the past. My advice to you would be to let go of this baggage and focus on your life in the present. Pay attention to all the positives that you have now. Towards the end of the month, your health and vitality will be at their peak. You could be working rigorously on achieving your fitness goals. But ensure that while doing so you don't injure yourself, or overdo any routine if you have already sustained injuries.

May

You will be doing exceptionally well in May which will be marked by taking action for your health. But whatever you do, ensure you adopt a conservative attitude towards your health and respect your body's limits. Your health is likely to improve further as the month progresses. If you have been suffering from a serious health ailment, then you should get some respite this month. You may be confused about treatment options and a doctor's diagnosis at this time. This stage of research and introspection will be quite difficult but you will receive the answers you are seeking. Even a ten-minute walk alone to introspect will produce some clarity and help you take a decision.

June

You will be feeling restricted and constrained and unable to do what you want to do. This is not a good situation to be in and you should try to break free from it. The best way to do this is to be optimistic. Mid-month, you will begin to recover from the deficits in your health. Your recovery will be rapid and you will be in for some positive news related to a test report you have been expecting. The key to good health lies in these daily activities. You will need to keep up your effort in the forthcoming months to stay fit and healthy and have an overall sense of well-being.

July

You will be on a break this month. You may take this break to relax and unwind and get some clarity in your thinking, or the break could be for hospitalization. Whatever the reason, this break will serve you well and give you some time to relax. Your health conditions are a manifestation of your negative thoughts which typically emerge because of stress and tension. I see you strategizing and chalking out plans to move ahead and set goals in health. A woman may come along and help you in health matters. She could be a healer or an instructor of some kind.

August

You need to be careful about who you trust in health matters. Someone may not be entirely honest with you about your condition. If you suspect foul play, get to the bottom of it. In the case of medical treatment, get a second opinion on the intervention suggested. Stay vigilant. The good news is that despite the odds, your health will recover. You will heal from your old wounds and your chronic ailments will see some improvement. You will manifest your greatest dream in health towards the end of month. This will leave you feeling happy and motivated for the new beginning that lies ahead.

September

You will need to change your attitude and your approach to health to keep up with the times. If you don't do this, your health may suffer. You may come upon a change which is difficult to deal with this month, and your only option will be to alter your lifestyle and your approach towards your body and mind. The good news is that this sacrifice will bring its own reward. You will receive this reward within a few days from the time you initiate this change. Your body and mind will start responding to your new approach and you will feel upbeat and healthier.

October

If you are confused about some issue about your health, your intuition will guide you in the right direction. This may not be the time to take any risky decisions or have a medical intervention which you are not convinced about. Remove all doubts before you commit to any intervention. You will have some happy times later in the month when you will be relaxed and at peace. You may decide to go on a holiday or a vacation to rejuvenate. This will be an excellent decision considering the emotional upheaval you faced recently.

November

If you have any questions related to your health, know that the answers lie in your past. Take a walk down memory lane and deal with the repressed emotions from your childhood. Processing these emotions will help heal your old wounds. Dig deeper and you may find the answers to many of your emotional issues. Towards the end of the month, you may put an end to an association that has failed to work out for you. This could involve a healer, doctor or an instructor. This could also imply a sudden end to a relationship related to love, work or wealth. You could be feeling distraught and hopeless because of this decision, but this end will eventually give you some respite and present you with a solution to your problem.

December

A woman, who may be part of your health scene this month, will help you achieve your desired outcomes. As you progress to the end of the month, you will be ready to adopt a new approach to your health. I see you establishing a health routine which includes eating a balanced diet, getting enough sleep and exercising daily. Along with this daily routine, you should also adopt a more serious approach towards developing your emotional health and achieving an overall sense of well-being. This is an excellent way to end the year. However, I see that you may unleash your indulgent side in the last few days of December.

Wealth Forecasts

January

The year will not start well for you. You may be deceived or cheated by someone you trusted with your money or wealth planning. There is also a possibility that a minor theft may take place in the early part of the month. Don't trust people so easily and keep in mind that someone somewhere is not being honest with you. You will have to do a thorough investigation before you decide to make an investment based on another person's judgement and guidance.

You will initiate something new in terms of an investment plan or a start-up venture with an intention to make money. This is unexplored territory for you; hence it will come with some risks and challenges. But what's exciting about this plan is that beyond its risks and challenges lie big rewards.

February

Your returns on investment will be good and the other aspects of your wealth will also be performing well. There will be a perfect balance in the way you conduct your finances, and you will know exactly where your money is going and where you need to use it. Mid-month, a woman may help you out with your financial planning. She will offer you some information which may change the course of your finances. You should also leverage your creative skills at this time which could lead to some interesting ideas and open the door to greater opportunities for wealth generation.

March

Contracts and legal agreements which promise better prospects will be headed your way. You will have enough money as long as you balance your income and expenditure. I see that you may lose track of your spending which will cause a slight imbalance. You will be able to correct the imbalance which will cause your financial situation to improve towards the end of the month. Money will come through one way or the other. This will be a great time to earn money through investments. If you have the appetite for taking risks, then in my opinion you should take a leap into the stock market now.

April

You will take up a new financial avenue this month. This will be in the form of a joint venture or a collaboration of some kind, or you may join hands with another person or institution for financial gains. However, do look out for the middle of the month when your finances may take a beating. Your situation will improve towards the end of the month and you will have enough to take care of your own expenses and those of your family members. You should consider saving some part of your earnings for future contingencies. The best way to attract money to yourself is to give out as much as you can with the intention to give, and not to gain from this.

May

This will be a very good month for your finances and you will strike the right balance between your income and expenses. You may consider big-ticket purchases like a home or announce a wedding or an engagement which will lead to expenses that you will comfortably manage. I see you getting lucky and receiving a windfall at the end of the month. This unexpected sum of money will come through sheer luck, family inheritance, gambling or some other source.

June

You will meet a financial adviser who will provide you with some financial insights that will help you plan better. Mid-month, you may be thinking too much about the things you don't have and can't afford instead of focusing your energy on what you already have. This kind of pessimism will only lead to negative experiences. If you have a certain financial goal in your mind, then chalk out a viable plan and work on achieving it. Don't simply sit back and procrastinate it. In the last few days of the month, you will be eagerly awaiting the returns on your investments or money from some other source.

July

You may feel constrained and unable to do the things you want to do financially. You may begin to detest your financial situation. Instead of adopting this negative approach, stay positive and look at what you have and what you are capable of earning in the future. Moderate your expenses to match your income. Towards the end of the month, you will need to face the reality of your financial situation. The news will not be good and you will have to face the music. The best way to reverse this financial downturn will be to freely give what you have. This giving will attract much more to you.

August

There will be an unexpected change in your financial situation this month which will sweep you off your feet. This change may cause an upheaval in your financial planning. It will end an ongoing association or plan which seemed worthwhile and consistent, and begin a new one. The more you think about the past, the more you will push the good away. You should look at ways to salvage the present situation rather than brood over what has gone by. The month will end with some positive news which you have been waiting for. This breakthrough, which took a long time coming, will be a reality this August. I see you on an upward path and proceeding towards financial stability.

September

You should seek financial guidance from an expert or a professional this month. One such individual or institution will offer you reliable financial advice which will ease your mind. Your money situation will get better and you will be on your way to financial stability. You will have enough money to cover your expenses and more will come from unexpected sources. This may be through a family inheritance, a lottery or gambling. Mid-month, you will be brooding over what you don't have instead of focusing on what you do have. The best way to change your negative mindset is to adopt an attitude of gratitude for everything you possess now.

October

I see you eagerly awaiting some reward or a return on investments. But this windfall is going to take longer than you anticipated. The money will come when the time is right. The answers to your financial problems lie in your past. I see something emerging from your past, an old memory, an old contact or a past association which will lead to some interesting opportunities. This blast from the past holds the key to a treasure trove. You must use it and cash in on the opportunities that could transform your life.

November

If you think your financial difficulties are here to stay, and persist with such negative thoughts, what you fear may become a reality. The good news is that despite your pessimism, you will achieve a balance between your income and your expenses. The temptation to overspend will be quite strong towards the end of the month. You may be tempted to splurge, but this could disturb your financial equilibrium.

December

The financial block that you have been facing will dissolve and money will begin to come in gradually once again. However, don't get carried away by your earnings and avoid lavish spending. You should use this influx prudently. In mid-December, you may begin to worry about managing your expenditure. This is the time to take action to release funds which seem stuck. For instance, if you are in a business, increase your collections and if your finances depend on someone else's decision, gently put pressure on this person so that you get what you want. This is the time to act fast.

I see some positive developments at the end of the month, when you will get the financial assistance you have been waiting for. This will open the doorway to financial betterment and opportunities that could transform your situation.

Career Forecasts

January

You will need to be more organized and balanced in your approach to your work this month. A man, someone senior and in a position of authority, will mentor you through this phase. He will take a liking for your work and will want to support you in the best possible way. Your work will become challenging and the people around you will be difficult to deal with. I see you inclined to give up and flee the situation. But this will be a cowardly move especially after you have come so far. In my opinion, you should hang on and prove you are up to the challenge. You will reap the rewards for your efforts at the end of the month in the form of money and recognition for all the effort you have put in.

February

You will hear some positive news that will lift your spirits and boost your morale. But don't take your work so seriously that you forget to have fun. The middle of February will be a golden period for you. I see you exceptionally happy with the way your career has panned out. In fact, this phase is so positive that any wish you make for your career may just come true. I see good news coming your way but it will come with some delay. If you were expecting this news at the end of the month, then in all likelihood you will be disappointed. You may have to wait a little longer for this news to arrive.

March

You will take up a new job, an assignment, a project or a client this month. This is a new beginning; and of course, it will come with its challenges and risks. While it may appear to be adventurous and promising, it will have some teething problems. You will be excited to prove yourself and will be ready to do whatever is required in this regard. Mid-month, you may face small issues such as a co-worker scheming against you. You need to focus on your job and brush away these petty issues. Sometimes it's good to take a walk down memory lane. When you do this, you may happen across something or someone who will strike the right chord and a life-changing career opportunity will be presented to you.

April

A woman will come along and play an important role in your career, pointing you in the right direction for success. This is an important time to stay focused and convert your thoughts into action. Mid-month, you will be eagerly awaiting an opportunity or a good break which you are certain will come through. The month will end on a positive note. You will get what you want which will leave you overjoyed. You will be emotionally ready to take on what life presents next.

May

You will receive accolades for achieving your targets and deliverables this month. You will be assisted by a woman whom you can trust. People will be impressed by your achievements and begin to take notice of your work. There will be a general buzz around you. If you feel underpaid for the amount of work you have been doing, then you should speak up and ask for a raise. A man, who may appear to be a bully but is actually just doing his job, will create difficulties for you towards the end of the month. You may be taking what he says and does personally.

June

You will be doing exceptionally well in your career and your work will be noticed by everyone. You will be enthusiastic because of some developments you are expecting in the near future. This could be a job change, a job offer or some other positive news in your existing set-up. You should consider using your creative skills to make a difference to your career this month. A woman may help you in executing this impossible feat. Remember if you respect and appreciate what you do, your work will respect you back.

July

You will start something remarkable this month, such as a new venture, a job or an assignment which is exciting but also has some risks. You will embark on a journey which is different, unexplored and something beyond the mundane. During this time, stay aloof from office politics and don't pay too much attention to people who try to create an impediment to your progress. Your work will eventually speak for you. There will be a delay in some opportunity or good news which you have been eagerly awaiting. It will come but in its own sweet time. During this trying time, avoid stepping on people's toes. Getting desperate or forcing people to take a decision favourable to you will only push your luck away.

August

You will be your own greatest adversary this August. The situation could get difficult for you and your co-workers in general will let you down. They will disregard your work and try to steal the accolades due to you. However, negative thoughts and resentment towards these people will only make the situation worse. Don't let these personal remarks pull you down so much that you begin to create problems for yourself. Calm down and see the situation improve. The month will end with some positive developments, and these instances will only increase if you begin to approach your work less seriously and learn to have some fun.

September

You may undertake international travel and explore opportunities which could give you an international placement. Your work will be on an upswing and I see you happy and completely in harmony with your work. You have a thrilling adventure ahead of you and there is a lot you can learn and enjoy from this experience. Towards the end of the month, you will be serious about your work goals and will be ready to execute the tasks assigned to you. At some point you will realize that you are capable of success and that you will achieve victory against all odds.

October

You may face some sort of defeat this month. The people around you may disregard and disrespect your work and steal your thunder. This will leave you disheartened and stressed. Mid-month, you will be eagerly waiting for decisions or opportunities that depend on other people. Unfortunately, there will be some delay in these, and your patience will be tested. The month will end with some amount of boredom arising in your work. You will lose interest and may begin to see only the negative aspects of your career. Instead, if you focus on the bright side of your career, you may attract what you desire.

November

You will have to take some difficult decisions which will involve ending your association with an ongoing job, client or project. You could consider relocating for a better job or career prospect. This will be a good decision in the present scheme of things. Later in the month, you could be stuck in a situation of imbalance where you are torn between two aspects of work. This may mean two jobs, two people or two assignments which will begin to take their toll on you. You have the energy to handle only one of them. So make a quick choice and move on. The month will end in a phase with your work situation getting difficult. You may be overwhelmed, tired and may feel defeated and would be considering giving up all that you have earned so far to escape this gruelling phase.

December

This December, you will reap the rewards for all the hard work you put in last month. You will witness positive outcomes and the situation at work will improve. If you are looking for work, then a good offer will come through this month. I see you juggling your work with your personal life to achieve work–life balance. Towards the end of the month, when you look back at the year gone by, I see that you may have feelings of regret and remorse. In my opinion, you should drop this emotional baggage which has become an impediment to your progress. It is important that you start the new year with a clean slate.

Acknowledgements

This book is a product of my hard work, and my knowledge of and dedication to tarot. I would like to thank the universe for giving me this opportunity for the third time to bring the magical power of tarot to you in the form of this book. My mission is to make tarot a household name and the universe has helped me in every aspect to achieve this. I would like to thank my beloved husband, Manoj Nair, for his support and my daughter, Miara, for her patience and love. They are my pillars who have supported me to become what I am today. Finally, I would like to thank my publisher, HarperCollins, for giving me this brilliant opportunity to bring forth the magic of tarot to you through this book. One other important person who has helped me with my books is Bidisha Srivastava. Her relentless coordination has taken my books across the seven seas. This book is a product of our efforts. I hope you enjoy unravelling your future through it.